The Efficiency of New Issues Markets

First published in 1992, *The Efficiency of New Issue Markets* provides a theoretical discussion of the adverse selection model of the new issue market. It addresses the hypothesis that the method of distribution of new issues, has an important bearing on the efficiency of these markets. In doing this, the book tests the efficiency of the Offer for Sale new issue market, which demonstrates the validity of the adverse selection model and contradicts the monopsony power hypothesis. This examines the relative efficiency of the new issue markets and in turn demonstrates the importance of distribution in determining relative efficiency. The book provides a comprehensive overview of underpricing and through this assesses the efficiency of new issue markets.

T0268714

The Efficiency of New Issue Markets

Kyran McStay

Routledge
Taylor & Francis Group

First published in 1992
by Garland Publishing Inc.

This edition first published in 2017 by Routledge
2 Park Square, Milton Park, Abingdon, Oxon, OX14 4RN
and by Routledge
711 Third Avenue, New York, NY 10017

Routledge is an imprint of the Taylor & Francis Group, an informa business

Publisher's Note
The publisher has gone to great lengths to ensure the quality of this reprint but points
out that some imperfections in the original copies may be apparent.

Disclaimer
The publisher has made every effort to trace copyright holders and welcomes
correspondence from those they have been unable to contact.

A Library of Congress record exists under LCCN: 92034079

ISBN 13: 978-1-138-57490-8 (hbk)
ISBN 13: 978-1-138-57492-2 (pbk)
ISBN 13: 978-1-351-27304-6 (ebk)

THE FINANCIAL SECTOR
OF THE AMERICAN ECONOMY

EDITED BY
STUART BRUCHEY

A GARLAND SERIES

THE EFFICIENCY
OF NEW ISSUE MARKETS

KYRAN McSTAY

GARLAND PUBLISHING, INC.
NEW YORK & LONDON
1992

Library of Congress Cataloging-in-Publication Data

McStay, Kyran P.
    The efficiency of new issue markets / Kyran McStay.
        p.   cm. — (The Financial sector of the American economy)
    Includes bibliographical references and index.
    ISBN 0-8153-0966-X (alk. paper)
    1. Stocks—Prices—United States. 2. Stocks—Prices—United
States—Mathematical models. I. Title. II. Series.
HG4915.M47   1992
332.63'222'0973—dc20   92-34079
                                                                CIP

To Jacqueline and my parents

Contents

Chapter 1

The Efficiency of New Issue Markets: Introduction

	Introduction	1
I.	Alternative Explanations of Under Pricing	2
	Monopsony Power and Inefficiency	3
	The Adverse Selection Model	5
II.	Empirical Evidence on Under Pricing	7
	Under Pricing and the Distribution of Initial Returns	8
	Initial Returns and Uncertainty: Empirical Relationship	9
	Distinguishing Between the Alternative Hypotheses	10
III.	Preview	11
	Theoretical Developments of the Adverse Selection Model	11
	Distribution and Efficiency	13
	Testing the Efficiency of the Offer for Sale	15
	Distribution and Efficiency: Evidence from US and UK	16
	Summary and Conclusion	17

Chapter 2

The Adverse Selection Model of the New Issue Market

	Introduction	18
I.	Modifications to the Adverse Selection Model	19
	The Assumption of Risk Neutrality	19
	Comparison with Rock's Model	19
	The Structure of the Model	20

II. Uninformed Demand   23
     Utility Maximisation   23
     The Adverse Selection Bias   24
     Determining Uninformed Demand   25
     A Necessary Condition for an Uninformed Bid   26
     The Uninformed Demand Function   27
     Bounds on the Offer Price   28
     Rock's Restriction on Uninformed Demand   29

III. The Optimum Offer Price: The Issuer's Behaviour   29
     The Expected Revenue Function   30
     What is the Optimum Discount?   31
     Is Discounting Rational? A Necessary and Sufficient
     Condition   32
     The Rationality of Under Pricing: the Uniform Distribution 33
     Numerical Examples   34

IV. Implications of the Adverse Selection Model   35
     Expected Return for Uninformed Investors   35
     The Expected Return from Underwriting   36
     Uncertainty and Initial Performance   38
     The Effect of Informed Demand   39

V.   Further Developments of the Adverse Selection Model   40

Chapter 3

Distribution and the Efficiency of New Issue Markets

     Introduction   46

I.   The Economics of "Bunching" Selling Arrangements   48
     The Central Selling Organisation of the De Beers Group   48
     Essential Aspects of the Bunching System of Distribution   51

II. Bunching in the New Issue Market   51
     Eliminating the Adverse Selection Bias by Bunching   52
     The Importance of the Method of Distributing New Issues   55
     Modelling the Preferential Allotments to Uninformed   57
     The Role of Under Pricing with Bunching   59

III. Institutional Arrangements in UK and US   59
     The Offer for Sale   59
     The Placement of the London Stock Exchange   60
     The IPO in the US   61

Testing the Importance of Distribution   64

Chapter 4

Testing the Efficiency of New Issue Markets

    Introduction   66

I.   Testing the Efficiency of New Issue Markets   67
    Zero Expected Returns to Uninformed Investors   67
    Zero Expected Returns from Underwriting   68
    Testing Efficiency of the Offer for Sale   69

II. Evidence on Under Pricing from the UK   70
    The Distribution of Initial Returns in the UK   70
    The Demand Function for New Issues   71
    The Relative Magnitude of Informed and Uninformed
    Demand   72
    The Risk Neutrality Assumption   73

III. The Expected Returns for the Uninformed Investor   74
    Estimating Expected Return for the Uninformed   74
    Testing for Zero Expected Returns for the Uninformed   75
    Interpreting the Zero Expected Return Equilibrium   75

IV. Efficient Underwriting Markets   76
    Estimating the Expected Cost of Under Subscription   76
    The Size of the Underwriting Concession   77
    Testing for Zero Expected Returns for Underwriters   77

Chapter 5

**Distribution and the Efficiency of New Issue Markets
in the US and the UK**

    Introduction   84

I.   Estimating the Uncertainty-Under Pricing Trade-off   85
    Ranking issues by Uncertainty   86
    Estimating the Uncertainty-Under Pricing Trade-off   87

II. The Relative Efficiency of New Issue Markets   88
    Uncertainty-Under Pricing Trade-off for Offers for Sale   88
    The Uncertainty-Under Pricing Trade-off for Placements   89
    The Uncertainty-Under Pricing Trade-off for the IPO   90
    Summary and Conclusion   90

Chapter 6
Summary and Conclusions   96

Appendix 1
**The Nature of the Information Asymmetry
in New Issue Markets**

     Introduction   98
I.   The Adverse Selection Model When the Informed do not
     have Perfect Information   99

Appendix 2
Mathematical Appendix

I.   Mathematical Appendix to Chapter 2   106
II. Mathematical Appendix to Appendix 1   112

Appendix 3
Hot Issue Markets

     Introduction   116
I.   Uncertainty-Under Pricing Trade-Off in Hot Issue Markets   117
II. The Hot Issue Market of 1980: Natural Resource Issues   118
III. Conclusions   119

Bibliography   121

Index   124

Illustrations

Table 2.1	Comparison of the Principal Differences Between the Current Model and Rock's Model	41
Table 2.2	List of variables	41
Figure 2.1	Partial Uninformed Demand Equilibrium: pl < p < po	42
Figure 2.2	The Full Uninformed Demand Equilibrium	42
Figure 2.3	The Critical Price pf	43
Figure 2.4	The Partial Demand of the Uninformed with no Discounting when Informed Wealth is less than Issue Size: $p = E[V]$	43
Figure 2.5	The Full Subscription Equilibrium: $p = pl$	44
Figure 2.6	The Uninformed Demand Function	44
Figure 2.7	The Expected Revenue Function	45
Figure 4.1	Distribution of Adjusted Initial Returns for 238 Offers for Sale during 1971-80	79
Figure 4.2	Scatter Diagram of Initial Returns vs Number of Times Subscribed	80
Figure 4.3	Distribution of Adjusted Initial Returns for 238 Offers for Sale During 1971-80 Weighted by the Probability of Receiving Allotment	81
Table 4.1	Average Uninformed and Informed Demand	82
Table 4.2	Mean Initial Return and Initial Return Weighted by the Probability of Receiving an Allotment	83

Table 4.3   The Expected Percentage Loss From
                 Underwriting (Excluding the Underwriting
                 Concession)   83

Table 5.1   Regression Model of the Initial Performance
                 of the Offer for Sale: 1971-1980   91

Table 5.2   The Uncertainty-Under Pricing Trade-off
                 for Offers for Sale in the UK   93

Table 5.3   The Uncertainty-Under Pricing Trade-off
                 for Placements in the UK   94

Table 5.4   Ritter's Estimates of the Relationship between
                 Initial Performance and a Proxy for Uncertainty   95

Table A.3.1   The Uncertainty-Under Pricing Trade-off for
                 IPOs in the US: Hot Issue Market Effects   120

Table A.3.2   The Uncertainty-Under Pricing Trade-off for
                 Natural and Non-Natural Resource Issues   120

Acknowledgments

I would like to thank my dissertation committee, Proff. Michael R. Darby, chairman, Prof. Benjamine Klein and Prof. Sheridan Titman for their help in the preparation of this thesis. I would also like to thank the Trinity Trust, An Bord Scolaireachtai Comalairte, Fulbright, the University of California and the Sloan Foundation for financial support during my graduate education.

I would also like to thank Paddy Waldron of Trinity college, Dublin for his considerable help with the mathematics contained in chapter 2 and for many other useful comments and suggestions.

Chapter 1

The Efficiency of New Issue Markets:
Introduction

Introduction

The most striking anomaly concerning the operation of new issue markets is the apparent under pricing of unseasoned common stock offerings. The term under pricing refers to the observation that the initial performance of unseasoned new issues is, on average, significantly positive. Initial performance is usually measured by the change of the closing share price on the first day or first month of trading relative to the initial offer price. The observation of positive average initial returns on a randomly chosen group of new issues suggests that they are offered at an expected discount relative to the price which is established in after market trading. The average initial performance of SEC-Registered unseasoned common stock issues is generally in the range of 15 to 20 percent with the standard deviation of initial returns in the 30 to 40 percent range. The existence of positive initial returns has been taken as *prima facia* evidence of the inefficiency of new issue markets.

The aim of this thesis is to shed further light on the subject of the under pricing and thereby assess the efficiency of new issue markets. There have been many non-rigorous explanations advanced for under pricing which amount to no more than the statement that "new issues are under priced to assure the success of the issue". Ibbotson (1975) cites some of these—for example, an explanation "prevalent in Wall Street" is that "under pricing new issues 'leaves a sweet taste in investors' mouths' so that future underwritings from the same issuer could be sold at attractive prices" (Ibbotson 1975, p 264). To date there have been only two internally consistent and rigorous explanations offered to account for under pricing. The first is based on a long held belief of the exploitation of monopsony power by the investment banking industry: investment banks individually, or in collusion, exploit the inexperience of issuers and under price unseasoned offerings. The second line of research, which is of more recent origin, is based on the specification of an information asymmetry whereby some investors have better information—less uncertainty—concerning the valuation of the issue than others. This uneven distribution of information gives rise to an adverse selection bias against unsophisticated or lesser informed investors. This research is due to the pioneering work of Rock (1982, first published in 1986).

The intuition behind the adverse selection model of the new issue market is the following: there is a group of informed investors who have superior abilities at recognising issues which will decrease in price in initial trading. These investors, who are likely to be professionals with access to equity research, apply only for issues which they assess to be undervalued at the offer price. As a result unsophisticated investors face a higher probability of receiving an allotment in issues which are overvalued. New issues are, therefore, under priced to compensate the unsophisticated investor for the bias in the probability of allotment between good and bad issues.

This chapter examines the alternative explanations of under pricing (section I) and reviews existing empirical evidence relating to the pricing of unseasoned common stock offerings (section II). Section III outlines the research contained in this thesis.

I.   Alternative Explanations of Under Pricing

The monopsony power and adverse selection hypotheses are the only theoretically consistent explanations of under pricing which have been offered to date. This thesis takes the adverse selection hypothesis as the maintained hypothesis and the monopsony power hypothesis as the alternative hypothesis.

Monopsony Power and Inefficiency

The following argument is typical of the monopsony power explanation of under pricing: investment banks individually, or in collusion, exploit inexperienced issuers by under pricing. The gains are passed onto investors in return for side payments: the investment bank rations shares in over subscribed issues to its regular clients and receives a side payment in the form of higher charges for the other services which it provides. Adherents to this view point to the widespread use of side payments in the investment banking/securities industry: for example, many services, such as research, are provided on a 'soft dollar' basis, where costs are recouped from security dealing charges. Ibbotson (1975) discusses various monopsony power explanations. Baron (1982) provides a rigorous formulation of the monopsony power hypothesis.

Baron's model is essentially a model of the demand for investment bank advising and distribution services based on information asymmetries between the issuer and the bank. The bank is better informed than the issuer about capital market conditions and the issuer cannot observe the distribution effort of the bank. The advising function has value since the issuer can delegate the pricing decision to the bank so that it uses its superior information about capital market conditions. Distribution effort has value to the extent that the bank can increase the demand for the issue. The term delegation contract is used for the contract under which the issuer engages the bank to price and distribute the issue.

The problem faced by the issuer is to choose the optimum delegation contract given rational expectations about the bank's incentive to mis-represent its information about capital markets and its incentive to shirk in its distribution effort. The optimum delegation contract involves the investment bank choosing an offer price below the first best offer price—defined as the price which the issuer would set if it knew the investment bank's information had and if it could observe distribution effort. Investment banks will, however, under price new issues in order to economise on distribution effort thereby increasing the expected return from new issues activity. From the issuer's perspective, this equilibrium is superior to that where the it does not employ the services of the bank to price the issue since it gains some advantage from the bank's information and distribution effort—intuitively, the issuer is better off being exploited by the investment bank when compared with the case where it does not employ the investment bank.

Baron demonstrates that the value to the issuer of delegating the offer price decision is an increasing function of the issuer's uncertainty about the market demand for the issue and that the offer price chosen by the bank is a decreasing function of this uncertainty: the greater the bank's information advantage the greater the extent of under pricing. As Baron's model hypothesises, the bank's information advantage about the demand for the issue and capital market conditions is positively related to the uncertainty of the issuer so that the extent of under pricing is also related to uncertainty.

There are several conceptual difficulties with the monopsony power explanation of under pricing. The first lies in the findings of many studies which point to the competitive nature of the investment banking industry (see for example Hayes (1971,1979) and Hayes et al (1983)). Also, one of the longest anti-trust trials in history failed to find any evidence of collusion between 17 of the largest investment banks in the US (see Medina 1953). Judge Medina concludes in his opinion:

> If they had in fact acted in combination or as a unit to divide the business among themselves, and to form a monopoly vis-a-vis the other firms in the industry, as alleged, the pattern of such combination, no matter how cleverly disguised or concealed, must surely have emerged, after such a long and continuous scrutiny as has gone on in this case for almost three years. But it did not. (Medina 1953 pp. 415-6)

To ensure survival in such a competitive market the investment bank must balance the desires of issuers and investors—provided that exploitation of issuers' inexperience is detectable. Under pricing resulting from exploitation is unlikely to survive in a competitive investment banking industry since information on the extent to which new issues are under priced becomes public information. An investment bank could establish a reputation of not exploiting the issuer by excessive under pricing and thus increase its market share. Beatty and Ritter find "that investment banks pricing off the line [of average under pricing] in one sub-period do in fact lose market share in the subsequent period, although the relation is a noisy one." (1986 p. 227)

Another difficulty encountered by the monopsony power hypothesis is found in the fact that the pattern of under pricing appears to have been unchanged since the regime of fixed security dealing commissions ended in the US in May 1975. One of the more convincing explanations of why the investment bank should pass on the gains from under pricing to investors was that they received side payments in the form of higher than competitive security dealing charges. There is no evidence to suggest that the extent of under pricing has decreased despite the large falls in dealing expenses which have occurred since fixed commissions were abolished in the US in May 1975 (see Ritter 1984).

A further observation which casts doubt on the monopsony explanations is that under pricing exists even where the initial public offering is made by competitive tender (see Dimson (1979) and Jacquillat and McDonald (1978)). This illustrates that under pricing is a feature of the competitive operation of new issue markets. Investment banks generally set the offer price at a level where there is some excess demand given the orders submitted—for example, for the Offer for Sale by tender for Morgan Grenfell (summer 1986) the strike price was set at a level were the issue was about four times over subscribed. Despite this fact the issue realised negative initial returns.

To date there has been only one attempt to explain the role of under pricing in a competitive market for investment banking services. This explanation is contained in the adverse selection model developed in Rock (1982 and 1986).

The Adverse Selection Model

The adverse selection model of the new issue market assumes that the issuer and the investment bank are uncertain about the share price which will be established in after market trading. The problem created for the organisation of the new issue market is that some investors have superior information about the value of the firm. These investors apply only for issues which they believe are undervalued at the public offer price. The investors who do not have superior information apply for all issues or at random with respect to the realised initial return for the issue.

Uninformed investors, therefore, face a bias in the probability of allotment for "good" and "bad" issues: issues which experience positive initial returns will be more heavily subscribed than those with negative initial returns because of the selective participation of informed investors. The uninformed will face a higher probability of allotment for bad issues—reflecting the lower demand—than for the good issues. In this case if all issues were offered at their expected value—that is, they are not under priced—the expected return to the uninformed investor would be zero.

The central hypothesis of the adverse selection model of the new issue market is that issues are under priced on average to compensate the uninformed for the bias in the probability of allotment between good and bad issues: the expected gain from under pricing compensates the uninformed for the expected loss associated with adverse selection. Dimson (1979) recognised this point in the introduction to his thesis but it was Rock (1982) who provided the first formal modelling of the theory.

In Rock's formulation of the market for initial public equity offerings the issuer and investment bank are uncertain about the true value of a share, v, but produce an unbiased estimate which is a random drawing from the distribution f(v). The issuer must set an initial offer price, p, and solicit orders at that price. The offer price may not be changed in the light of realised demand. Rock's model is based on the following main assumptions:

1.   Informed investors have perfect information about v and apply only for issues which are undervalued (ie. v > p); and

2.   Allotment is by lottery—orders are drawn at random and filled in their entirety until there are either no more orders (the issue is under subscribed) or no more shares (the issue is over subscribed). All investors, informed or uninformed, face the same probability of allotment assuming that they apply. There is no preferential rationing to any group of investors;

Under these assumptions, the uninformed face a higher probability of allotment in the bad state than in the good state when the informed participate in the market. Consequently, without under pricing, the average returns to the uninformed are negative. Rock demonstrates that there exists an expected discount which compensates for this bias. For the case where f(v) is uniformly distributed the model yields the conclusion that the issue price is set at the level for which uninformed demand equals issue size—the optimum offer price is the full subscription price.

The main testable implication of the adverse selection model which has been implemented to date is the prediction of a positive relationship between the uncertainty of the investment bank concerning the price which will be established in after market trading and average under pricing. This hypothesis is developed in Rock (1986), Ritter (1984) and

Beatty and Ritter (1986). Adverse selection imposes losses on the uninformed because the probability of being allotted shares in the bad state is higher than the probability in the good state. The greater the uncertainty the higher the probability that large losses will be incurred as a result of mis-pricing by the issuer, therefore, the greater the amount of under pricing required to compensate the uninformed.

The main thrust of Rock's theoretical analysis was to demonstrate that there always exists an expected discount or amount of under pricing which is sufficient to compensate the uninformed for the adverse selection bias created by the presence of uninformed investors. Rock does in fact establish this point. The intuition behind this assertion is that the issuer could always give the shares away for virtually nothing in order to attract the participation of the uninformed.

Rock also demonstrates in a numerical example of his general model that under pricing may be a rational strategy for the risk averse issuer. However, because of the fact that Rock's model is so complicated, he is not able to examine the factors which determine whether it is rational for the issuer to under price. Chapter 2 presents further theoretical refinements of the adverse selection model which enable a more thorough examination of the rationality of the under pricing equilibrium from the perspective of the issuer. This work and the other research contained in this thesis is reviewed in section III. The next section provides a review of existing empirical evidence concerning under pricing and the efficiency of new issue markets.

II. Empirical Evidence on Under Pricing

This section reviews existing empirical evidence concerning the pricing of initial public offerings of common stock and discusses whether existing evidence helps to distinguish between the competing explanations for under pricing. Of the many studies which have examined under pricing this review pays particular attention to only four since these provide a exhaustive description of the available evidence and because there is a high degree of conformity of these results with other studies. The studies reviewed are Securities and Exchange Commission (1963), Ibbotson and Jaffe (1975), Ibbotson (1975) and Ritter (1984).

Under Pricing and the Distribution of Initial Returns

Ibbotson and Jaffe (1975) examined the initial performance of all unseasoned common stock issues (initial public offerings (IPO)) registered with the Securities and Exchange Commission for the period 1960 through 1970 and reported an average initial performance, adjusted for movements in the market index, of 16.8%. Ritter (1984) extended the Ibbotson and Jaffe sample to include all the SEC-Registered offerings from 1960 to 1982 and found an average initial return of 18.8% for the sample of over 5,000 offerings. The average initial return for all offers for sale conducted on the London Stock Exchange between 1971 and 1980 was 7.43%. For Placements on the London Stock Exchange during this period the average is 15.5%. See chapters 3 and 5 for a discussion of the relative magnitude of under pricing in the US and the UK. This research is the first which has provided a thorough analysis of the relative efficiency of new issue market in different countries.

Ibbotson and Jaffe (1975) and Ibbotson (1975) present further evidence concerning the distribution of initial returns: the distribution of initial returns has a significantly positive mean (in the 15 to 20 % range), it is positively skewed (median is approximately 5% below the mean), has large standard deviation (approximately 35%) and is highly peaked. The distribution of initial returns for a sample of new issues from the UK, presented as figure 4.1 in chapter 4, demonstrates a high degree of conformity with the findings for the US.

In the Ibbotson (1975) study the initial performance is positive in 66 of the 112 randomly selected issues. A test of significance leads to the conclusion that it is not possible to reject, at a 5% significance level, the null hypothesis that there is an even chance of observing a positive initial performance. However, evidence presented by SEC (1963) strongly suggests that investors have a better than average chance of drawing an issue with positive initial performance. Of 1,671 unseasoned common stock issues registered with the SEC (including those under Regulation-A) during the years 1959 to 1961, 1,327, or 79.5% traded at a premium immediately after trading commenced. Table 1.1 presents the distribution of initial returns for the issues in the SEC sample. For the sample of UK offers for sale examined in chapter 4, 156 of the 238 issues (65.5%) realised positive initial performance. The asymptotic t-test leads to the conclusion that the null hypothesis, that there is an even chance of observing positive initial performance, is rejected.

An interesting feature of table 1.1 is the difference in the distribution of initial returns between the fully registered issues and those registered under Regulation-A. Only 14.9% of Regulation-A issues realised price declines in initial trading while 23.8% of fully registered issues realised negative initial performance. Conversely at the other end of the distribution only 4.8% of the fully registered issues experienced initial returns over 100% as against 10.2% for Regulation-A issues. This evidence is consistent with the proposition that as uncertainty increases the size of the expected initial performance also increases since the Regulation-A issues are usually speculative start-up ventures.

All of these features of the distribution of initial returns point to the fact that the investment bank forms an estimate of firm value and offers the shares to the public at an expected discount.

A further interesting feature concerning the pattern of under pricing is its variability over time. Ritter (1984) presents evidence which illustrates the existence of cycles in average initial performance and new issue volume. Periods of higher than average initial performance have been referred to as 'hot issue' markets. An explanation for these hot issue markets, which was provided by Ritter, is discussed in the following section dealing with the empirical relationship between uncertainty and the extent of under pricing.

Initial Returns and Uncertainty: Empirical Relationship

Ritter (1984) establishes the existence of a positive relationship between certain proxies for uncertainty and the average amount of under pricing. The proxies considered are (1) annual (constant dollar) sales in the most recent 12-month period prior to flotation, taken as a proxy for the degree of establishment of the firm and (2) the daily standard deviation of the stock price during the first 20 days of trading. The results, using the standard deviation proxy, are summarised in table 5.4.

Ritter (1984) also attempts to explain the hot issue market of 1980 as an equilibrium phenomenon caused by (1) a stationary positive relationship between uncertainty and expected initial performance and (2) a changing risk composition of initial public offerings. Specifically Ritter argues that hot issue markets are observed when there is a higher than average fraction of new issues which are in the high-risk category. Despite uncovering evidence of a strong relationship between under pricing and uncertainty, Ritter is unable to account for the 1980 hot issue market entirely on the basis of a changing risk composition of new issues. Evidence presented suggests that the higher than average initial returns are the result of a non-stationarity in the initial returns of natural resource issues: the average initial returns for natural resource issues during the hot issue period were 5 times greater than usual, even after allowing for possible changes in the risk composition of these issues. Ritter also finds that the average initial returns of the non-natural resource issues during the hot issue period were of a broadly similar magnitude, in relation to the chosen proxies, when compared to the average for issues prior to the hot issue period. The explanation of the hot issue market is discussed further in an appendix to chapter 5.

The estimation of the uncertainty-under pricing trade-off forms an important part of the empirical analysis of this thesis. A methodology for estimating the relationship is derived in chapter 5. Comparisons of the magnitude of the relationship in different new issue markets forms the basis of the assessment of relative efficiency of these markets.

Distinguishing Between the Alternative Hypotheses

Ritter (1984) and Beatty and Ritter (1986) interpret support for the positive relationship between uncertainty and initial performance as support for the adverse selection model of the new issue market. This relationship alone, however, does not provide a way of conclusively distinguishing between the adverse selection and monopsony power hypotheses since the existence of such a relationship is implied by both explanations, as discussed above (see also chapter 2 section II). However, the Beatty and Ritter finding that investment banks which under price issues more than average lose market share is difficult to reconcile with the monopsony power hypothesis.

Rock (1982) provides an alternative test of the proposition that informed investors participate in new issue markets: if some investors have superior information about the realisation of the after market price then shares with positive initial returns should be completely sold out and the syndicate account closed more quickly than issues with negative initial returns. If, however, investors have homogenous expectations, the length of the selling period should be uncorrelated with initial performance. Rock finds a strong positive relationship between the length of the selling time for best-efforts underwritings and initial returns and therefore rejects the hypothesis of homogenous expectations:

that is, he concludes that informed investors participate in initial public offerings.

This finding is suggestive of the fact that some investors have better information than others, however, it is also consistent with a rather naive view that share price is simply a function of excess demand and not a reflection of fundamental information concerning value. Ibbotson's (1975) finding of after market efficiency, however, presents evidence against the "naive" excess demand hypothesis—Ibbotson finds no evidence that the positive initial returns are eliminated in after market trading.

Furthermore, neither of these test is capable of addressing the issue of whether new issue markets are efficient. It is possible that both the adverse selection and monopsony power hypotheses provide partial explanations of under pricing. This thesis produces the most conclusive evidence to date in favour of the adverse selection model and provides a test which is capable of distinguishing between the two hypotheses. The test exploits information on the demand for each issue which is available for offers for sale on the London Stock Exchange.

III.   Preview

There are two main strands to this thesis, each comprising of a theoretical chapter and an empirical chapter. The theme connecting each of the elements of this research is the efficiency of new issue markets for initial public offerings of common stock. The first examines the adverse selection hypothesis as developed by Rock and provides a test of the hypothesis using the Offer for Sale on the London Stock Exchange. The second develops a role for distribution in determining the relative efficiency of new issue markets and tests this hypothesis by exploiting institutional and regulatory differences between the US and the UK.

The theoretical issues relating to each of the elements of the thesis are contained in chapters 2 and 3. The remainder of this section provides a brief introduction to each chapter.

Theoretical Developments of the Adverse Selection Model

The aim of chapter 2 is to provide further theoretical developments of the adverse selection model developed by Rock (1982 & 1986) and to develop explicit testable implications which can distinguish between the adverse selection and the monopsony power explanations of under pricing. The model in chapter 2 also provides the theoretical context for the analysis of distribution in chapter 3.

Shortcomings of Rock's model which this chapter addresses are:

1.   Complexity: The complexity of the model is due to the fact that investors are assumed to be risk averse. Considerable simplification is attained by making the risk neutrality assumption;

2.   The model provides a general analysis of the behaviour of the uninformed investor but it does not address in a thorough way the issue of whether or not it is rational for the issuer to under price. It merely demonstrates in a numerical example, for a risk averse issuer that under pricing is rational. The simplification attained by the risk neutrality assumption enables a general description of the behaviour of the issuer to be derived. This produces several interesting insights about the under pricing equilibrium and the rationality of under pricing from the issuers perspective.

3.   Rock imposes restrictions on the relative magnitude of informed and uninformed wealth: specifically he assumes that informed wealth is less than issue size and that informed wealth is arbitrarily large. The assumption that informed wealth is less than issue size is contradicted by the empirical analysis of demand for new issues in chapter 4. Rock imposes these restriction for analytic tractability. The simplification afforded by the risk neutrality enables assumption a complete description of the model—including a necessary and sufficient condition for under pricing to be rational for the issuer— without imposing restrictions on the relative demand of the different classes of investor's.

Thus the theoretical advances of the adverse selection model stem mainly from the simplification gained from the risk neutrality assumption. The justification for the assumption is that the risk that an issue is mis-priced is weakly related to systematic or market related risk and can therefore be controlled by diversification provided that the investor is compensated for the expected value of the loss arising from the bias in the probability of allotment between good and bad issues. Chapter 4 presents evidence supporting this proposition.

This chapter also develops testable implications of the adverse selection model which can be used to distinguish between the competing explanations of under pricing. These are the equilibrium conditions of zero excess returns to uninformed investors and to underwriters.

The analysis in chapter 2 illustrates an important qualification to the validity of the adverse selection model as specified here and in Rock. Specifically it is demonstrated that, for the case where the distribution of the bank's estimate of the firm value is uniform, it will never be rational for the issue to under price when informed demand is greater than twice issue size—that is, the expected revenue without under pricing is greater than the expected revenue with under pricing. The qualification is raised by the fact that estimated informed demand is on average significantly larger than twice issue size.

It is hypothesised that the likely solution to this difficulty lies in the recognition that in actual new issue markets informed investors do not have perfect information about the value of the issue. In this case there will be instances where the "informed" share in the losses of the uninformed by causing rationing when the issue is overvalued thereby reducing the extent of the adverse selection bias against these investors. An appendix to chapter 2 discusses the adverse selection model where the informed do not have perfect information but instead also produce an estimate of firm value like the investment bank.

Distribution and Efficiency

The distribution function implied by the adverse selection model is reduced to a simple clerical function: the investment bank simply rations shares in proportion to excess demand among all investors who apply for the issue. Initiation (or certification) and underwriting may by important economic functions performed by the bank but distribution, by itself, is not an important function.

Previous literature on investment banking has long recognised the importance of the role of distribution (see, for example, Davey (1976), Cooke (1962), Stewart (1949) and Waterman (1958)). To date, however, there has been no theoretically satisfactory explanation of the economic function performed by investment banks in distributing new issues. Does distribution form an important part of the role of the investment bank in making primary markets for new issues—why does the issuer not simply announce the issue, with the recommendation and certification of the investment bank, and allow investors apply directly for the shares? The fact that the issuer generally pays half of the gross spread of the investment bank syndicate as selling commission suggests that distribution is an important stand-alone function: Members of the selling group receive the commission, from the IIB, for shares actually sold.

It is argued in chapter 3 that a possible role for the investment bank in distribution is enforcing a rationing scheme which assures preferential allotments to uninformed investors and thus reduces the transactions difficulties created by the uneven distribution of information in the market. The marginal return for distribution in syndicated IPOs in the US is about half of the gross spread paid to the syndicate—the selling concession is paid independently of the underwriting concession.

The theory of the distribution function performed by the investment bank is based on a model of distribution which enforces "bunching" as a means of controlling wasteful or costly quality search when pre-purchase quality information is expensive to produce. The particular model examined, which draws on the literature dealing with the economics of information, is that developed by Kenny and Klein (1983) to explain the operation of the De Beers' Central Selling Organisation. This model when applied to new issue markets illustrates the incentive for investment banks to ration shares in a preferential manner to their regular clients who behave as uninformed investors. Such a distribution system is shown to reduce the extent of the adverse selection bias against these investors and consequently the amount of under pricing required to induce their participation.

This chapter also develops a test of the proposition that the method of distribution has an important bearing on the efficiency of new issue markets by exploiting institutional and regulatory differences between the US and the UK. The markets chosen are the "Offer for Sale" and "Placement" new issue markets in the UK and the "Initial Public Offering" (IPO) new issue market in the US. The hypotheses tested are:

1.   The Offer for Sale is the least efficient new issue market because investment banks are prohibited from rationing in a preferential manner to regular clients;

2.   The Placement new issue market is more efficient than the Offer for Sale because the investment bank is not restricted to ration shares in proportion to excess demand among all investors; and

3.   The IPO is the most efficient because investment banks can ration in a preferential manner and because the syndication system of distribution is more developed in the US than in the UK.

Testing the Efficiency of the Offer for Sale

Chapter 4 provides a test of the adverse selection model developed in chapter 2 using a database of new issues conducted by the Offer for Sale in the UK. Two features of the Offer for Sale make it uniquely suited to testing the efficiency of new issue markets:

1.   The method of allotment is similar to that assumed in the adverse selection model: The regulations of the London Stock Exchange require that over subscribed shares are allotted among all investors in relation to total demand—that is, the investment bank is prohibited from adopting a system of preferential allotments to regular clients. It follows, therefore, that the efficiency conditions developed in section II of chapter 2 provide the appropriate benchmark for assessing the efficiency of this new issue market.
2.   The realised level of demand for each issue becomes public information: The London Stock Exchange requires the investment bank to publish information on the total demand as a means of policing the required allotment procedure.

The Offer for Sale provides a unique opportunity for testing the absolute efficiency of new issue markets since it is possible to explicitly test the equilibrium conditions predicted by the adverse selection model for this market. It is not possible to test these equilibrium conditions for other new issue markets since the probability of allotment for the uninformed for over subscribed issues cannot be estimated given that the extent of preferential allotments cannot be easily estimated.

This chapter test the equilibrium conditions of zero excess returns to the uninformed and to underwriters. The chapter also: provides estimates of informed and uninformed demand; tests the appropriateness of the risk neutrality assumption made in deriving the equilibrium conditions; and estimates the shape of the demand function for new issues. The chapter presents the most conclusive evidence offered to date in favour of the adverse selection model and the efficiency of new issue markets.

Distribution and the Efficiency: Evidence from the US and the UK

This chapter presents a test of the proposition that the method of distribution has an important bearing on the relative efficiency of different new issue markets. The Offer for Sale new issue market provides a useful benchmark against which to assess relative efficiency since: 1. Stock Exchange regulations prohibit preferential allotments to regular clients of the investment bank; and 2. the test of the Offer for Sale new issue market present strong evidence in favour of the adverse selection model and the efficiency of this market.

The test of the relative efficiency is based the assessment of the amount of under pricing in each new issue market. However, since the average amount of uncertainty differs from market to market—because of institutional and regulatory features discussed in chapter 3—it is necessary to base this assessment on the estimation of the uncertainty-under pricing trade-off for each market: one new issue market is defined as being more efficient than another if, for a given increase in uncertainty, there is a smaller increase in the average amount of under pricing.

Section I of this chapter develops a methodology for estimating the uncertainty-under pricing trade-off. The estimation difficulty is that there is only a single observation on initial performance for each issue. A grouping methodology is therefore employed to estimate the expected discount and the uncertainty of the investment bank concerning the price which will be established in the after market. The basis approach is to:

1.   Rank issues by proxies for uncertainty and to divide the issues into groups;
2.   Estimates of the expected amount of under pricing and uncertainty are obtained as the mean and standard deviation of the initial returns for the issues within each group; and
3.   Estimate the uncertainty-under pricing trade-off by fitting a simple linear regression between these group estimates.

Section II presents the estimates of the uncertainty-under pricing trade-off for the Offer for Sale and Placement new issue markets in the UK and the IPO new issue market in the US. The results provide strong support for the hypothesis the method of distribution has an important bearing on the relative efficiency of new issue markets.

An appendix to this chapter applies this methodology to the analysis of the hot issue market of 1980. This issue was studied by Ritter (1984).

Summary and Conclusion

In summary, therefore, the main developments and conclusions of the research reported in this chapter are:

1.   The further theoretical development of the adverse selection model of the new issue market;
2.   The hypothesis that the method of distribution of new issues has an important bearing on the efficiency of these markets;
3.   The test of the efficiency of the Offer for Sale new issue market which demonstrates the validity of the adverse selection model and contradicts the monopsony power hypothesis; and
4.   The test of the relative efficiency of the different new issue markets which demonstrates the importance of distribution in determining relative efficiency.

Table 1.1   **Distribution of Registered and Exempt Unseasoned Common Stock Offerings by Initial Performance: 1959-1963**

Initial Returns	All Issues	Registered	Regulation-A
Greater than 100%	6.8%	4.8%	10.2%
50% to 100%	13.3%	11.0%	17.4%
25% to 50%	17.5%	17.0%	18.6%
0% to 25%	41.8%	43.4%	38.9%
Less than 0%	20.5%	23.8%	14.9%
Number of Issues	1,671	1,073	598
Median	21.0%	18.0%	25.0%

Note: The table is compiled from information contained in table IV-30 of SEC (1963, p. 621). The median initial return, which refers only to 1961, is taken from SEC (1963, p. 516).

Chapter 2

The Adverse Selection Model
of the New Issue Market

Introduction

The critical aspect of the adverse selection model of the new issue market is the assumed information structure: the issuer's knowledge of share value, v, is limited to the probability density function f(v). However, there is a group of investors, termed informed, who have perfect information about v. The uninformed (all other investors) do not produce an independent point estimate of v but have sufficient information to determine that it is a random variable from the distribution f(v).

This information structure is the most simple way of modelling the situation where some investors have privileged information about the issue relative to other investors. Despite the simplified information structure it has been necessary to impose further important restrictions in order to make meaningful deductions from the model. Rock's solution was to impose restrictions on the relative wealth of the informed and uninformed investors. Specifically, Rock assumes that:

1. Informed wealth is less than the expected value of the issue, I < E[V].Z, and
2. Uninformed wealth is arbitrarily large: that is, the number of uninformed investors tends to infinity.

An empirical analysis of the Offer for Sale in the UK provides evidence against the appropriateness of the assumption that informed demand is less than the issue size (see chapter 4). This chapter develops an alternative specification of the adverse selection model in which it is unnecessary to place restrictions on relative wealth to reach a description of the under pricing equilibrium. It is, therefore, possible to explicitly examine how the equilibrium attained varies with the relative wealth of the two classes of investors and to derive a necessary and sufficient condition for under pricing to be rational for the issuer.

I.   Modifications to the Adverse Selection Model

The Assumption of Risk Neutrality

The simplification of the model contained in this chapter is based on the assumption that investors are risk neutral with respect to the losses caused by adverse selection. This assumption is a reasonable representation of investor behaviour if the risk that the issue is incorrectly valued is unrelated (or weakly related) to systematic or market related risk. In this case the uninformed can diversify the risks arising from the mis-priced issues provided that they are under priced on average to compensate for the expected value of the losses caused by the bias. The risk neutrality assumption is not, therefore, inconsistent with the proposition that investors require higher returns (relative to the riskless asset) for risks which cannot be controlled by diversification.

The empirical analysis in chapter 4 supports the proposition that the risk that an issue is incorrectly priced is only weakly related to movements in the market index: movements in the market index statistically explain only a small proportion of the initial returns for new issues (see (4.3) and (4.4) in chapter 4).

Comparison with Rock's Model

The principal differences between the model presented in this chapter and that developed by Rock arise from the simplification gained by assuming that investors and the issuer are risk neutral. This simplification enables a more complete mathematical description of the model than the case for risk averse investors. Table 2.1 provides a comparison of the principal differences between the two models.

The simplification afforded by the risk neutrality assumption enables a richer set of conclusions to be drawn from the model. As a result of these simplifications it is possible to:

1.   Derive a general expression for the optimum discount—
        independent of the form of the distribution f(v)—and show that
        where discounting is rational the offer price will always be set
        at the full subscription price: that is, the price where
        uninformed demand equals issue size;
2.   Demonstrate that Rock's restriction that informed demand is
        less than issue size is sufficient to guarantee the rationality of
        the under pricing equilibrium;
3.   Derive a general necessary and sufficient condition for under
        pricing to be a rational strategy for the issuer—this expression
        depends on the form of the distribution and the size of informed
        demand relative to issue size;
4.   Examine this condition for the case where v is uniformly
        distributed and show that in this case it is not rational to under
        price if informed demand is greater than twice issue size;
5.   Discuss the conclusion concerning the rationality of under
        pricing where informed investors do not have perfect
        information about v—that is where the extent of their
        information advantage is less than that implied by Rock's
        specification of the adverse selection model;
6.   Discuss the rationale for the relationship between uncertainty
        and initial performance which gives a clearer interpretation to
        the empirical relationship estimated in other studies;
7.   Discuss the version of the model where the level of informed
        demand is endogenously determined in relation to the expected
        gains to becoming informed and present a test against the
        alternative hypothesis that the level of informed demand is a
        purely random variable from issue to issue.
8.   Demonstrate a role for underwriting in the context of the
        adverse selection model of the new issue market.

The Structure of the Model

        The assumptions of the model are:
1.   The informed have perfect information about v while the
        uninformed are limited to the knowledge that v is drawn from
        the distribution f(v);
2.   There are two assets the riskless asset with a zero rate of return
        and a risky asset made available only through the issuer;

3.   The issuer and investors maximise the expected value of terminal wealth, W. Initial wealth, W_0, for all investors is normalised at unity;

4.   Allotment is by lottery and the issuer sells unsold shares in the after market at their true value v;

5.   The informed apply with their entire wealth if the offer price, p, is less than v;

6.   There are I informed and N uninformed investors;

7.   Uninformed wealth is larger than issue size;

8.   Borrowing and short selling are prohibited;

9.   Investors and the issuer have rational expectations; and

10.   The offer price must be set at or below E[V]—that is: the issuer/investment bank cannot consistently overprice the issue.

The rationale for the final assumption is the following: With risk neutrality the optimum strategy for the issuer is to set the offer price at infinity. The issuer would then sell the shares in the after market at their true value as assumed by the model—the derivation of expected revenue in section III assumes that unsold shares are sold in the after market at the true value. Thus, without imposing the above restriction there would be no new issue market—all shares would be sold in the after market. Chapter 3 provides insights in the role of the institutional structures in new issue markets. Table 2.2 sets out a list of variable definitions for this chapter.

The adverse selection model of the new issue market is examined in two parts:

1.   Determination of the distribution of total demand from the issuer's perspective—the demand side of the equation (section I); and

2.   Determination of the optimum offer price given the distribution of demand and the issuer's objective function—the supply side of the equation (section II).

The modelling strategy for examining the behaviour of uninformed investors is to focus on the level of the adverse selection bias—we examine the effect of adverse selection on the expected returns to the uninformed and demonstrate how their optimum level of demand is affected by this bias. The definition of the adverse selection bias used is b/b' where b is the probability that an investor receives an allotment in the state where the issue is undervalued—the good state—and b' is the probability of receiving an allotment when the issue is overvalued—the bad state. We define an increase in the adverse selection bias where b' increases relative to b—that is where b/b' decreases.

In this specification of the model informed demand is the only stochastic element of total demand—the level of uninformed demand at each offer price can be uniquely determined. The issuer is assumed to know the structure of the model which determines uninformed demand. Uninformed demand though non-stochastic is more difficult to model than informed demand. The analysis of uninformed demand, which is contained in section I, is made in three steps:

1.   Utility maximising behaviour given the offer price and assuming that the magnitude of the adverse selection bias is unaffected by variations in uninformed demand;

2.   Determination of the effect of uninformed demand on the adverse selection bias; and

3.   The equilibrium demand of the uninformed assuming that they have rational expectations of the degree of the adverse selection bias.

We will combine these three elements into a simple graphical analysis to illustrate the equilibrium level of uninformed demand. Given these steps it is a relatively simple matter to demonstrate that there always exists a price which will induce the uninformed to participate in the new issues market—this condition holds for all levels of informed relative to uninformed demand. The intuition is that the issuer could always "give the shares away" in order to attract the uninformed.

In order to determine whether it is rational to under price the issue it is necessary to examine the behaviour of the issuer—given the distribution of the demand function for the issue what is the optimum offer price for the issuer. Section III of this chapter is devoted to this discussion. There are several objective functions which can be assumed for the issuer. In an example of the determination of the optimum offer price (for the case where f(v) is uniformly distributed) Rock assumes that the issuer is risk averse and maximises the expected utility of terminal wealth. The risk aversion assumption is based on the proposition that the issuer will have a large portion of his wealth tied up in the firm. In this model necessary and sufficient conditions are derived for under pricing to be an optimum strategy even for the risk neutral issuer: that is, the condition which assures that expected revenue with under pricing is larger than the expected revenue without under pricing.

To review briefly, the structure of this chapter is as follows: Section II examines the behaviour of the uninformed. Section III examines the behaviour of the issuer. Section IV examines testable implications which are used in the extensive testing of the adverse selection model in chapter 4 using a sample of new issues on the London Stock Exchange. Finally, section V is devoted to the consideration of further developments of the adverse selection model.

II. Uninformed Demand

Utility Maximisation

The first part of the analysis of the behaviour of uninformed demand is to define their objective function. It is assumed that the uninformed investor maximises the expected value of terminal wealth, $E[W]$, where, as demonstrated in theorem 2.1 of the mathematical appendix,

$$E[W] = 1 + (T/p)E\{V\text{-}p\,|\,A\}P\{A\} \qquad (2.1)$$

$$E\{V\text{-}p\,|\,A\}P\{A\} = E\{V\text{-}p\,|\,V\text{>}p\}bP\{V\text{>}p\}+E\{V\text{-}p\,|\,V\text{<}p\}b'P\{V\text{<}p\}$$

That is, $E[W]$ is equal to initial wealth, unity, plus the expected return on the number of shares allotted, $(T/p)E\{V\text{-}p\,|\,A\}P\{A\}$, since the return on the riskless asset is assumed to be zero.

Assuming risk neutrality it is easy to demonstrate that there is a critical level of the adverse selection bias such that the uninformed investor will be indifferent between all possible levels of demand for the issue. At this critical level the expected return from new issue subscription is zero so that the uninformed investor is indifferent about all possible bids. When the extent of the bias is greater than this critical level the uninformed will not apply for the issue.

The relationship between the utility maximising bid and the level of the adverse selection bias is illustrated by the L-shaped function in figure 2.1. The following discussions are made clearer by alerting the reader to the scale used on the y-axis of figure 2.1. The y-scale shows the adverse selection bias measured as b/b'—that is, the probability of allotment in the good state divided by the probability of allotment in the bad state (this scaling is chosen so that b/b' falls in the range [0, 1]). Thus when we talk of an increase in the adverse selection bias we mean a decrease in b/b'—the adverse selection bias decreases moving up the y-axis.

If instead investors were assumed to be risk averse the curve defining the relationship between the optimum bid and the adverse selection bias would be upward sloping—the uninformed would require a higher expected return for taking the added risk of increasing their demand, therefore, *ceteris paribus*, they will increase their bid only if the adverse selection bias is reduced. With risk neutrality we do not have to consider this factor. This is where the simplification of the model is achieved.

The proof of the relationship between the utility maximising uninformed bid and the level of the adverse selection bias with risk neutrality is demonstrated in the following manner: from 2.1 it follows that $E[W]$ is maximised at $T=0$ when $E\{V-p \,|\, A\}P\{A\} < 0$. $E[W]$ is maximised at $T=1$—that is, the uninformed apply with all their wealth—where $E\{V-p \,|\, A\}P\{A\}>0$. When $E\{V-p \,|\, A\}P\{A\} = 0$ the uninformed are indifferent about all possible levels of demand. The critical level of the adverse selection bias for which $E\{V-p \,|\, A\}P\{A\} = 0$ is derived from (2.1) as:

$$b_o(p) \;=\; \frac{E\{p\text{-}V \,|\, V<p\}P\{V<p\}}{E\{V\text{-}p \,|\, V>p\}P\{V>p\}} \qquad\qquad (2.2)$$

The properties of $b_o(p)$, which are required in the demonstration of the theorems in this chapter, are derived in theorem 2.2.

The Adverse Selection Bias

This outline of investor behaviour takes no account of the effect of uninformed demand on the adverse selection bias. The equilibrium bid of the uninformed must take account of the effect, on the bias, of informed demand and variations in the level of uninformed demand. It is assumed that the uninformed have rational expectations of the extent of the bias—that is, their expectations about the extent of rationing in each outcome are consistent with experience. Therefore, to derive the uninformed demand function it is necessary to examine the relationship between T and b/b' given I. This relationship is illustrated in figure 2.1 by the v-shaped curve.

The adverse selection bias can be defined in terms of maxima and minima as follows

$$b/b' = \min\{1, \max\{pZ/(NT+I), NT/(NT+I)\}\} \quad (2.3)$$

As b/b' increases, the extent of the adverse selection bias decreases: that is, the probability of allotment in the favourable state increases relative to the probability of allotment in the unfavourable state. The definition of b/b' has three branches as follows,

1.   No rationing in either state as uninformed and informed demand combined, NT^*+I, are insufficient to cause rationing. In this case b=b'=1;

2.   Only undervalued issues rationed as uninformed demand alone, NT^*, is insufficient to cause rationing—however, $NT^*+I > pZ$. In this case b'=1 and b/b' = pZ/(NT+I). This branch of the function b/b'(T) is decreasing in T—that is, larger bids by the uninformed **increase** the extent of the adverse selection bias; and

3.   Rationing in both states since $NT^* > pZ$. In this case b' = pZ/NT and b = pZ/(NT+I) so that b/b' = NT/(NT+I). In this range b/b'(T) is increasing in T.

Determining Uninformed Demand

It is assumed that the uninformed determine their demand for the issue in a manner which is consistent with the actual probabilities of allotment is each state—that is, they have rational expectations about b/b'. This means that equilibrium uninformed demand is determined at the intersection of the $b_0(p)$ and b/b' functions in figure 2.1. It they demand less than this amount the adverse selection bias will be less than the critical level (assuming for the moment that the downward sloping portion of the v-curve is the relevant segment) and they will have the incentive to increase their demand (conversely if they demand a larger amount than implied by this equilibrium). The equilibrium demand of the uninformed is illustrated by T^* in figure 2.1.

It is evident from the relationships in figure 2.1 that several possible equilibria may arise:

1.   Zero demand by the uninformed (T=0): that is, b/b'(T) < $b_0(p)$ for all possible values of T. In this case the extent of the adverse selection bias is greater than the level at which the

uninformed are indifferent about participating in new issues market;

2.   Partial demand by the uninformed (0<T<1): only the second branch of the b/b'(T) function intersects the $b_o(p)$ function. This is the situation illustrated in figure 2.1; and

3.   Uninformed investors apply with their whole wealth (T=1): that is, b/b'(1) > $b_o(p)$. It is possible in this case (as illustrated is figure 2.2) that b/b'(T) = $b_o(p)$ for one or two levels of T less than unity. This does not imply that there are three possible equilibria since at the full demand equilibrium the uninformed are earning supernormal profits (E[W] > 0 since E{V-p | A}P{A} > 0).

Define p_f as the price at which the uninformed just begin to apply with their full wealth. This equilibrium is illustrated in figure 2.3. It is clear that at p_f there is a discontinuity in uninformed demand—at the price just above p_f uninformed demand falls from 1 to T'.

Thus, in this model there are three possible unique equilibria. The intuition behind the first two is clear but the third possibility deserves further consideration. This equilibrium is dependent on the uninformed recognising that if they jump to applying with their whole wealth they can reduce the adverse selection bias by reducing the proportion of informed demand in total demand. This possibility, which has no obvious parallel in real new issue markets, is an extreme possibility which results from the risk neutrality assumption.

In the remainder of this chapter it will be assumed that the only possible equilibria are the zero demand and the partial demand equilibria. Uninformed investors are constrained from suddenly jumping to applying with all their wealth. Rock also recognises the possibility that uninformed demand could explode if the offer price is set sufficiently low.

A Necessary Condition for an Uninformed Bid

The above analysis of uninformed behaviour yields a necessary and sufficient condition for the uninformed to apply for the issue: the uninformed will apply for the new issue if the extent of the adverse selection bias at zero demand is less than the critical level at which they would be indifferent about whether or not they apply—that is, if

$$b/b'(0) \ > \ b_o(p) \qquad\qquad\qquad (2.4)$$

Substituting T=0 in (2.3) this condition becomes

$$g(p) < Z/I \quad \text{for } pZ < I$$

where $g(p) = b_0(p)/p$. There is always a price which satisfies this condition since, as demonstrated in theorem 2.3,

$$\lim_{p \to 0} g(p) = 0 \tag{2.5}$$

In fact, since g is a monotonic function there is a unique critical price above which uninformed demand is 0 and below which it is positive.

The intuition behind the conclusion that a discount always exists such that the uninformed can be induced to apply, irrespective of the relative magnitude of N and I and f(v), is that the issuer could "give the shares away for virtually nothing." This is as far as Rock developed the model in its general form. The remainder of his results are based on the assumption that f(v) is uniformly distributed. Because of the risk neutrality assumption we can proceed further in the general form.

The Uninformed Demand Function

In the range where the uninformed submit a partial bid for the issue (along the second branch of b/b'(T)) their demand function may be derived as follows: the equilibrium demand, T^*, satisfies the condition $b/b'(T^*) = b_0(p)$, that is,

$$b_0(p) = pZ/(NT^*+I)$$

This condition yields the equation for the uninformed demand function in the range where the uninformed are applying for the issue with a portion of their wealth as

$$T^*(p) = (Z/g(p)-I)/N \tag{2.6}$$

Since g(p) is an increasing function of p (as demonstrated in theorem 2.3) the uninformed demand function is negatively sloped. (See figure 2.6 for a graphical representation of the uninformed demand function.)

The comparative static analysis of a change in the offer price in terms of the diagrammatic analysis of the optimum uninformed bid are as follows: a decrease in p causes both the L-curve and the v-curve the fall however the L-curve falls faster than the v-curve so that as price falls T^* increases.

Bounds on the Offer Price

Before proceeding with the description of the optimum offer price in section II we will define bounds implied by the above analysis. Specifically, the optimum offer price must lie in the interval $[p_o, p_l]$ where p_o is the price at which the uninformed are just about to demand the issue and p_l is the price at which total uninformed demand equals issue size: that is, the full subscription price for which $T^* = p_l Z/N$. If the offer price is not set in this range it is set at $E[V]$.

The issuer will not set the offer price in the range $(p_o, E[V])$ since discounts of this magnitude are insufficient to attract the participation of the uninformed but merely serve to reduce the expected revenue from the informed. Similarly price reductions below p_l will always reduce total revenue since the uninformed are already applying for the entire issue.

The expression for p_o can be derived from the definition of $b/b'(T)$ contained in (2.3) as follows: the uninformed will begin to subscribe if:

$$b_o(p_o) = \min\{1, p_o Z/I\}$$

From theorem 2.2 $b_o(E[V]) = 1$ and since $g(p)$ is a monotonic increasing function in p, so that the solution g^{-1} exists, it follows that

$$p_o = \min\{E[V], g^{-1}(Z/I)\} \tag{2.7}$$

When uninformed demand equals issue size $(T^* = p_l Z/N)$, $b/b'(T^*) = p_l Z/(p_l Z + I)$ by substitution into (2.3). The expression for p_l is derived by substitution into the condition $b_o(p_l) = b/b'(p_l Z/N)$ as follows

$$1 = h(p_l) \tag{2.8}$$

where $h(p) = (b_o(p)/p)(p + I/Z)$. The solution p_l which solves $h(p) = 1$ exists and is unique since $h(p)$ is a monotonic increasing function in p. Defining the solution to $h(p)$ as h^{-1} we derive the expression for p_l as

$$p_l = h^{-1}(1) \tag{2.9}$$

The expression for p_l is independent of N—it is dependent on the distribution $f(v)$, which determines $b_o(p)$, and informed wealth per share I/Z. The following intuition supports this conclusion: when total uninformed demand equals issue size the total losses imposed as a result of the adverse selection bias are independent of T—as N increases $T(p_l)$ will decrease but $NT(p_l)$ remains unchanged. The amount of under pricing required to compensate for this fixed loss is therefore also independent of N.

Rock's Restriction on Uninformed Demand

Rock imposes the restriction that informed demand is less than the expected value of the issue $(I < Z.E[V])$. We can now examine the implications of this assumption. In this case the first branch of the bias function $b/b'(T)$ exists so that $b/b'(0) = 1$. In this case the uninformed will apply for the issue even at an offer price of $E[V]$. At $E[V]$ the uninformed will bid up to $(pZ-I)/N$ because at this point rationing is just beginning to take place in the state where the issue has been undervalued: that is, for $T < (pZ-I)/N$ there is no adverse selection bias against the uninformed. This equilibrium is illustrated in figure 2.4. It follows therefore that $p_o = E[V]$ when $I < Z.E[V]$. We will use this point below to demonstrate that Rock's restriction on informed demand is sufficient to guarantee the existence of an under pricing equilibrium.

III.   The Optimum Offer Price: The Issuer's Behaviour

The issuer chooses the offer price to maximise the expected value of his objective function conditioned on the distribution of total demand for the issue. Rock examined the case where the issuer maximises the expected utility of terminal wealth under the assumption that he is risk averse. This section develops a decision rule for a risk neutral issuer: that is, an issuer who maximises the expected revenue from the issue. Assuming risk neutrality, the issuer's offer price decision may be examined as follows:

1.   What is the optimum discount—assuming that discounting is rational? As discussed above if discounting occurs the optimum offer price must lie in the range $[p_l, p_o]$. It will be demonstrated below that expected revenue is maximised at p_l in this range:

that is, if discounting occurs the optimum offer price is always p_1 and uninformed demand will equal issue size; and

2.   Is discounting rational? The risk neutral issuer will offer the shares at p_1 only if $r(p_1) > r(E[V])$ where $r(p)$ is the expected revenue at the offer price p.

Before examining these issues it is necessary to derive an expression for the expected revenue function taking account of informed and uninformed demand.

The Expected Revenue Function

The expected revenue function, $r(p)$, over the range $[p_1, p_o]$ is composed of two elements:

1.   Expected revenue given that the issue is undervalued by the probability that the issue is undervalued; and

2.   expected revenue given that the issue is overvalued by the probability that the issue is overvalued.

That is, the expected revenue function is:

$$r(p) \;=\; E[r \,|\, p{<}V]P\{p{<}V\} + E[r \,|\, p{>}V]P\{p{>}V]$$

Revenue, when the issue is undervalued, is always equal to the value of the issue pZ assuming that informed and uninformed demand are sufficient to cause rationing of undervalued issues. However, in the range $[p_1, p_o]$ uninformed demand alone is insufficient to cause rationing. In this case revenue, given that the share is overvalued, is:

$$E[r \,|\, p{>}V] \;=\; E[NT^*(p) + V(Z{-}NT^*(p)/p) \,|\, p{>}V]$$

assuming that any unsold shares, $Z{-}NT^*(p)/p$, are sold in the after market at the true value, v. The expression for $r(p)$ in terms of the structural parameters N, I, and $f(v)$, which is derived in theorem 2.4, is:

$$r(p) \;=\; Z.E[V] - I\int_0^p (1-v/p)f(v)dv \qquad (2.10)$$

What is the Optimum Discount?

Having derived the expression for r(p) it is a simple matter to demonstrate that p_l is the optimum offer price assuming that discounting is rational. To demonstrate this point it is sufficient to note that:

$$r'(p) = I[(1/p^2)\int_0^p vf(v)dv] < 0$$

This is a necessary and sufficient condition for $r(p_l)$ to be a local maximum for the function r(p) in the range $[p_l, p_o]$. The local maximum in the range $[0, E[V]]$ must occur a p_l or $E[V]$ given the boundary conditions discussed in section I. Thus if discounting is rational the optimum discount is $E[V] - p_l$. Rock does not derive a general expression for the optimum offer price. It is the simplification afforded by the risk neutrality assumption which allows us to derive the expression for the equilibrium offer price—without imposing restrictions on the relative magnitude of informed and uninformed demand or on the form of f(v).

Since this is one of the important results of the adverse selection model it is useful to develop further the intuition behind this point—this is done by taking the full subscription price as the starting point and examining the implication of increasing the offer price. At the full subscription price p_f uninformed demand equals issue size—uninformed demand can always take-out the issue. If the issuer were to increase price above this point, say to p_+, some portion of the shares would not always be taken up by the uninformed. Suppose that x shares are not demanded by the uninformed as a result of the increase in the offer price. These x shares must be either sold to the informed or in the after market.

However, the expected revenue from the sale of these x shares is always less than p_+x since the informed will only purchase them from the issuer if $v > p_+$. The issuer can never sell the x shares in the after market at v when $p_+ < v$ because the informed always buy them at the offer price. The issuer never gets a higher price than p_+ for any shares that the uninformed don't buy but it can receive a lower price. It is this one-sided aspect of the behaviour of the informed which makes it rational, even for a risk neutral issuer, to under price.

This argument shows why increasing price above p_f reduces expected revenue. Since the argument applies equally at any price between p_f and p_o it follows that expected revenue falls as price is increases between these points. Therefore if under pricing is rational the issuer will always choose the full subscription price.

Is Discounting Rational? A Necessary and Sufficient Condition

A necessary and sufficient condition for under pricing to be a rational strategy for the issuer is:

> the expected revenue at the full subscription price is larger than
> the expected revenue assuming that no discounting occurs—
> that is, $r(p_l) > r(E[V])$.

This condition is effectively guaranteed by Rock's restriction on informed demand. It was demonstrated above that the condition $I < Z.E[V]$ implies that $p_o = E[V]$ and thus $r(p_o) = r(E[V])$. Since we have demonstrated above that $r(p_l) > r(p_o)$ it follows that the issuer will always offer the shares at a discount if $p_o = E[V]$. The equilibrium level of uninformed demand for p_l is illustrated in figure 2.5. The uninformed demand function and the expected revenue function for the issuer are presented in figures 2.6 and 2.7 respectively.

When $I > Z.E[V]$, p_o is less than $E[V]$. It is possible that p_o may be so far below $E[V]$ that $r(p_l) < r(E[V])$ so that the issuer will not offer the issue at a discount. In this case $(E[V]) > r(p_l) > r(p_o)$.

We will develop a necessary and sufficient condition for under pricing to be an optimum strategy for the issuer when $I > Z.E[V]$. It is important to consider this generalisation of the model in the light of the empirical findings concerning the relative magnitudes of informed and uninformed demand.

The necessary and sufficient condition is derived as follows: Since the issue is just fully subscribed at p_l it follows that $r(p_l) = p_l Z$. At $E[V]$ the uninformed do not participate in the issue so that, by substituting $T^* = 0$ line (1) of theorem 2.4 in the mathematical appendix,

$$r(E[V]) = Z\{E[V] - \int_{E[V]}^{\infty} (v-E[V])f(v)dv\} = Zp_c \quad (2.11)$$

Substituting the definitions for $r(E[V])$ and p_1 into the necessary and sufficient condition $p_1 Z > r(E[V])$ yields the condition $h^{-1}(1) > p_c$. Since the solution to h^{-1} exists and using the definition of $h(p)$ in (2.9) the necessary and sufficient condition for under pricing to be rational is

$$1 > h(p_c) = \frac{b_o(p_c)}{p_c}(p_c + I/Z), \text{ or}$$

$$I < \frac{Z.p_c}{j(p_c)} \quad (2.12)$$

where $j(p_c) = b_o(p_c)/(1-b_o(p_c))$. It is not possible to gain further insight into this necessary and sufficient condition and thus the rationality of under pricing unless the form of the distribution $f(v)$ is specified.

The Rationality of Under Pricing: the Uniform Distribution

In order to carry the analysis of the necessary and sufficient condition for under pricing further we assume that $f(v)$ is uniformly distributed: that is,

$$V \sim U(E[V]-a, E[V]+a)$$

As demonstrated in theorem 2.5, in this case

$$\frac{p_c}{j(p_c)} = E[V] + (1/3)E[V] + (4/9)(E[V]-a) > E[V]$$

That is, under pricing may be rational for the risk neutral issuer even if informed wealth is larger than issue size: that is, if $I > Z.E[V]$. However, $p_c/j(p_c) < 2.E[V]$ so that it is never rational to under price, at least in this formulation of the model, if $I > 2(Z.E[V])$. The critical level of informed demand at which under pricing is just rational is:

$$I = Z(E[V] + (1/3)E[V] + (4/9)(E[V]-a))$$

Unfortunately this finding is contradicted by the empirical estimates of informed demand in chapter 4: estimated informed demand is 8 times issue size yet the evidence clearly shows that new issues are under priced. It is unlikely that the solution to this difficulty lies in the re-specification of the distribution $f(v)$, for example, to the non-symmetric log normal distribution.

The most likely solution to this difficulty lies in recognising the fact that the informed do not have perfect information about the after market value of the issue. This point is discussed briefly in section V and more extensively in an appendix to this chapter.

Numerical Examples

We present some numerical examples of the model for the case where $f(v)$ is a uniform distribution. First we examine the critical level of I for which under pricing is just rational for different values of the variance of the distribution $f(v)$—that is, for different levels of uncertainty (in this case the variance of v is $a^2/12$). The results are as follows:

Uncertainty and the Critical Level of Uninformed

Measure of Uncertainty standard deviation of $f(v)$	Critical level of Uninformed Demand for discounting to become rational
5.0	1.43
10.0	1.29
15.0	1.18
20.0	1.09
25.0	0.93
30.0	0.87

This illustrates, for example, that with uncertainty of 10% under pricing is not rational for the issuer if informed demand is more than 1.29 times issue size.

Next we examine the effect of the level of informed demand and uncertainty on the optimum offer price. The analysis assumes that $E[V]=1$ so that an optimum offer price of 1 implies that discounting is not rational—that is, the expected revenue with no discounting is greater than the expected revenue at the optimum offer price.

Analysis of the optimum offer price
Informed demand relative to issue size (I/Z.E[V])

Uncertainty (SD of f(v))	0.000	0.500	1.000	1.500	2.000
0.05%	1.000	0.982	0.970	0.960	1.000
0.10	1.000	0.964	0.938	0.918	1.000
0.15	1.000	0.945	0.904	0.873	1.000
0.20	1.000	0.925	0.869	1.000	1.000
0.25	1.000	0.905	0.831	1.000	1.000

The table shows that discounting is not rational when informed demand is more than twice issue size and when there are no informed investors. It also illustrates that the size of the optimum discount is an increasing function of uncertainty and that at some point as uncertainty increases under pricing ceases to be a rational strategy for the issuer.

IV.   Implications of the Adverse Selection Model

This section contains a discussion of implications of the adverse selection model. We develop two equilibrium conditions which are implemented in chapter 4 to provide a joint test of the adverse selection model and the efficiency of new issue markets. The first of these concerns the expected returns to the uninformed and the second concerns the expected returns to underwriters. We also discuss additional testable implications which are implemented in chapter 4.

Expected Return for Uninformed Investors

The specification of the adverse selection model under risk neutrality assumptions produces the equilibrium condition of zero expected returns to uninformed investors. [Proof: On the downward sloping part of the uninformed demand curve, $b/b'(T) = b_0(p)$: that is, in equilibrium the level of the adverse selection bias is equal to the critical level at which the expected value of terminal wealth is unity—this implies a zero expected return to the uninformed since initial wealth is unity and the return on the riskless asset is zero.]

A risk averse issuer would require a positive expected return before being induced to participate in new issue markets. The rationale for the risk neutrality assumption is that since the risks that an issue is mis-priced can be controlled by diversification capital markets will not allow the uninformed a positive expected return for bearing these risks: that is, the uninformed investor is compensated only for the expected losses resulting from the bias.

Chapter 4 presents estimates of the expected return to uninformed investors and find strong support for the equilibrium predicted by the model for risk neutrality.

It is important to note that this equilibrium holds independently of the behaviour of the issuer. It is the result of the competitive behaviour investors. Even if the issuer/investment bank sets the offer price below that predicted by rational behaviour and the adverse selection model, competition by the uninformed for shares assures zero expected return. If the expected return were positive the uninformed would increase their bid to restore the equilibrium.

The test of the equilibrium condition of zero expected returns for the uninformed, which is conducted in chapter 4, demonstrates that the uninformed are on average compensated for the adverse selection bias and also that competition for shares in fact assures that the expected return to these investors is zero.

We develop a test of the rational behaviour of the issuer/investment bank predicted by the adverse selection model by developing the model to account for underwriting.

The Expected Return from Underwriting

The analysis of the pricing decision of the issuer in this chapter suggests that, where discounting is rational, the issuer sets the offer price at the full subscription price—that is, the price at which the level of uninformed demand equals issue size. This conclusion concerning the competitive behaviour of the issuer/investment bank may not be implemented as a testable implication of the adverse selection model because the conclusion is based on the assumption of non-stochastic uninformed demand. With stochastic uninformed demand it may be rational for the issuer/investment bank to set the offer price such that expected uninformed demand is larger than issue size.

However, it is possible to derive an alternative implication of the competitive determination of the offer price, as predicted by the by a more general specification of the adverse selection model, by examining the expected returns to underwriters.

Only with stochastic uninformed demand is it possible to specify a role for the investment bank in underwriting new issues. We have demonstrated that, where it is rational for the issuer to under price, the offer price will be set at the full subscription price—the price where total uninformed demand equals issue size. It follows, therefore, that with non-stochastic uninformed demand all issues will be fully subscribed. Overvalued issues will be exactly subscribed (uninformed demand equals issue size) and undervalued issues will be over subscribed given the participation of the informed. In this situation there is no role for the underwriter—the issuer will not pay to have the proceeds of the issue guaranteed by an investment bank since they are effectively guaranteed by setting the offer price at the full subscription price.

The possibility of stochastic uninformed demand can be introduced in this model by assuming that the number of uninformed investors which apply for the issue, N, is random. Specifically we assume that N is a random drawing from the distribution $g(n)$ with mean $\overline{N}$ and that N is independent of $(p - V)$—the uninformed are "truly uninformed".

We do not present a formal proof of the equilibrium for this model, however, the following brief discussion provides some indication of the effect of stochastic uninformed demand and the rationale for underwriting in the context of the adverse selection model.

The equilibrium in the model with non-stochastic uninformed demand involved setting p at the full subscription price pl so that uninformed demand equalled issue size: $NT^* = p_lZ$—suppose that N in this model equals N. Now suppose that with stochastic uninformed demand the issuer also sets the offer price at pl. The expected number of uninformed investors which apply is also N however the expected revenue from the issue will now be less than p_lZ—revenue is not increased above p_lZ when $N > N$ but is lowered when $N < N$.

Abstracting from underwriting for the moment, in this situation the issuer is faced with the choice of either maintaining p at p_l or reducing it below this level to induce a higher level of demand from each of the uninformed investors which apply—that is, the issuer may reduce the offer price to attract a higher level of expected uninformed demand. This will increase revenue when $N < N$ but will have no effect on revenue when $N > N$. It will therefore result in an increase in uninformed demand.

A test conducted in chapter 4 suggests that average uninformed demand is greater than issue size supporting the proposition that the issuer will lower the offer price when uninformed demand is stochastic.

With underwriting an investment bank guarantees the proceeds for the issuer. That is, the underwriter incurs the risk of stochastic uninformed demand. Issuers have a demand for underwriting where they are risk averse. The more risk averse the issuer the smaller the utility which will be attached to an given level of expected revenue from the issue. Therefore, the greater the value placed on underwriting. In competitive underwriting markets the costs of underwriting will be determined by the expected losses to the underwriter and not by the value of the expected utility gain to the issuer from underwriting.

If we assume that the risk that an issue is under subscribed independent of market movements—which is the case if under subscription arises from random uninformed participation—competition will ensure that underwriters are compensated only for the expected value of losses arising from underwriting since these risks can be controlled by diversification. We present evidence in chapter 4 that initial return are only weakly related to market movements and that underwriters are compensated only for the expected losses arising from underwriting.

The test of zero expected returns for underwriters provides a test of the competitive behaviour of the issuer/investment bank against the alternative hypothesis that the investment bank exploits the inexperience of the issuer by under pricing to increase its expected return.

Uncertainty and Initial Performance

Uncertainty in the above model is measured by the standard deviation of the distribution $f(v)$. It is not possible to describe the comparative static results for this variable without specifying the form of the distribution $f(v)$. Beatty and Ritter (1986) demonstrate a positive relationship between initial performance and uncertainty for the case where $f(v)$ is a uniform distribution (their model is not a rigorous formulation of the adverse selection model since equilibrium uninformed demand is not endogenously determined).

Beatty and Ritter offer the following intuition for the relationship (page 215-16): " Faced with a winner's curse problem, a representative investor will only submit purchase orders if, on average, the initial public offerings are under priced...[A]s the uncertainty increases, the winner's curse problem intensifies. Roughly speaking, there is more to loose as uncertainty increases..." Beatty and Ritter and Beatty (1984) find empirical support for this relationship and interpret it as support for the adverse selection model.

This explanation of the relationship between initial returns and uncertainty is not a useful explanation of the relationship predicted by the model. We will develop an alternative intuition for this proposition which makes more sense in interpreting the empirical relationship between these variables.

The adverse selection losses imposed on the uninformed are a reflection of the fact that the informed have an information advantage over these investors. If it is assumed that the extent of this information advantage increases with uncertainty the extent of the adverse selection losses and therefore the amount of under pricing required must also increase. This relationship is implicitly assumed if the informed are modelled as having perfect information and everyone else imperfect information characterised by $f(v)$ where uncertainty is defined as the variance of $f(v)$.

Thus the justification for the empirical relationship between uncertainty and under pricing is dependent on the assertion that as uncertainty increases the information advantage of the informed over the uninformed also increases. As discussed in chapter 1, if it is assumed that as uncertainty increases the extent of the investment bank's informational advantage, relative to the issuer, increases, it follows that a positive relationship between uncertainty and under pricing is also implied by the monopoly power hypothesis. We cannot therefore use this relationship to distinguish between the two theories of under pricing.

In chapter 4 we develop a methodology for estimating the uncertainty-under pricing trade-off and use this methodology for testing the relative efficiency of different new issues markets.

The Effect of Informed Demand

From the definition of the equilibrium offer price in (2.9) it follows that the size of the expected discount increases with informed demand per share, I/Z. [Proof: since $h(p) = g(p)(p+I/Z)$ is increasing in I/Z for all values of p it follows that $h^{-1}(x)$ is decreasing in I/Z for all values of x and in particular for $x = 1$. Thus the expected discount $E[V] - p_1$ is increasing in I/Z.]

As I/Z increases the extent of the adverse selection bias also increases—that is as I increases b/b'(T*(pl), pl) decreases. Proof: At pl

$$\frac{b}{b'(p_l)} = \frac{Z}{[Z+I/h^{-1}(1)]}$$

Since $h^{-1}(1)$ is decreasing in I (as proved above) it follows that $I/h^{-1}(1)$ is increasing in I. Therefore $b/b'(p_l)$ is decreasing in I.

V.   Further Developments of the Adverse Selection Model

One of the most important qualification of the validity of the adverse selection model concerns the conclusion about the level of informed demand for which it is rational for the issuer to under price. Specifically, we demonstrated that, where f(v) is uniform, it would be irrational to under price if informed wealth was greater than twice issue size (the exact magnitude of informed wealth for which this is the case is derived above).

The most likely solution to this difficulty lies in the recognition that the informed do not have perfect information about the after market value of a share. In this case with informed demand, of average size I, the expected losses imposed on the uninformed will be less than with a similar level of perfectly informed demand since the "imperfectly informed investors" will sometimes make an error in assessing the value of the issue and cause rationing when an issue has actually been overvalued by the issuer. That is, informed investors will share in the losses from overvalued issues when they make an error in assessing the value of the firm. If this is the case the total required compensation to the uninformed in the form of under pricing is reduced. Thus the possibility of finding a rational under pricing equilibrium with average informed demand of the size observed is increased.

An appendix to this chapter presents a limited discussion of the adverse selection model where the informed do not have perfect information about the value of the issue. In this model we assume that the informed make an independent assessment of share value and apply with all their wealth if their estimate is greater than issue size. We demonstrate that the greater the variance of the distribution of the informed investors estimate—that is, the smaller is their information advantage—the smaller are the losses imposed on the uninformed and therefore the smaller the amount of under pricing required to compensate them for the bias in allotment. This is as far as we go in advancing this explanation for the difficulty cited above.

Table 2.1 **Comparison of the Principal Differences Between the Current Model and Rock's Model**

New Model	Rock's Model
Attitude to risk: Issuer and investors are assumed to be risk neutral	Issuer and investors are assumed to be risk averse
Informed investors wealth: Unconstrained	Less than expected value of issue
Uninformed wealth: Greater than the issue size	Arbitrarily large
Distribution of f(v): None	Assumed that f(v) is uniform

Table 2.2 List of variables

W_0 informed and uninformed initial wealth—normalised at unity
W   investor's terminal wealth
N   no. of uninformed investors—total informed wealth
I   no. of informed investors—total informed wealth
T   uninformed investor's demand
T*   equilibrium uninformed demand
Z   number of shares on offer
p   offer price
V   "true" value of each share
A   event where investor receives an allotment
B   event where investor does not receive an allotment
b $P\{A|p<V\} = \min\{1, pZ/(NT+I)\}$
b' $P\{A|p>V\} = \min\{1, pZ/NT\}$

Figure 2.1   Partial Uninformed Demand Equilibrium: $p_1 < p < p_0$

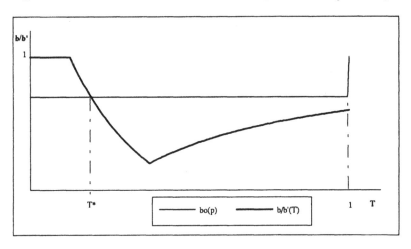

Figure 2.2   The Full Uninformed Demand Equilibrium

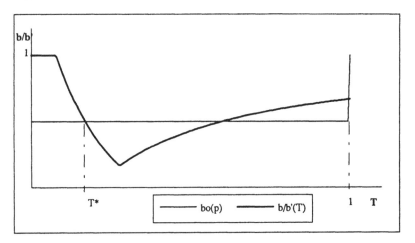

Figure 2.3   The Critical Price p_f

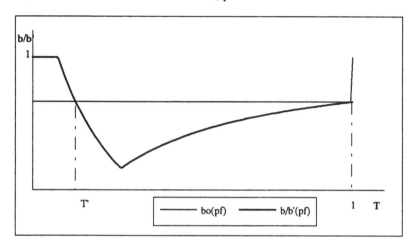

Figure 2.4   The Partial Demand of the Uninformed with no Discounting when Informed Wealth is less than Issue Size: p = E[V]

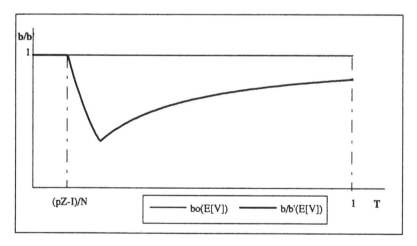

Figure 2.5   The Full Subscription Equilibrium: p = p₁

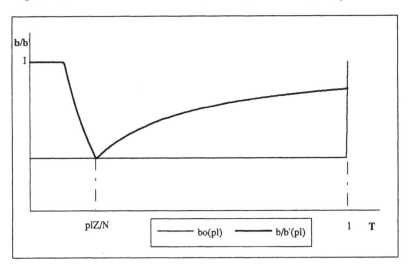

Figure 2.6   The Uninformed Demand Function

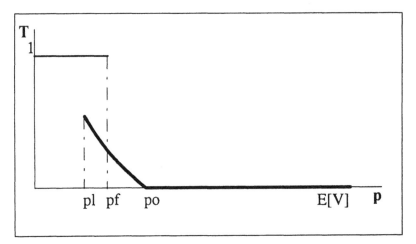

Figure 2.7   The Expected Revenue Function

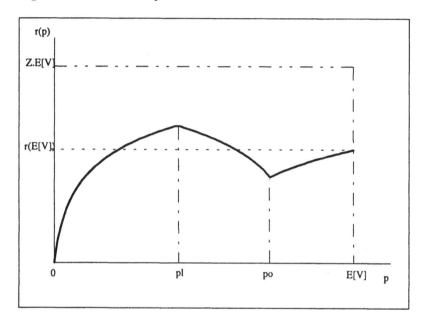

Chapter 3

Distribution and the Efficiency of
New Issue Markets

Introduction

The aim of this chapter is to examine the role of distribution in new issue markets. Previous literature on investment banking has long recognised the importance of distribution to primary capital markets (see, for example, Davey (1976), Cooke (1962), Stewart (1949) and Waterman (1958)). To date, however, there has been little or no satisfactory economic research explaining the role of distribution. The economic analysis of investment banking has concentrated on the underwriting and initiation (or certification) functions of the investment bank. Yet the largest component of the gross spread paid to the investment bank syndicate is the selling concession: the typical division of a gross spread of 2% is 0.25% for the initiating investment bank for certification, 0.75% underwriting commission and 1.0% selling commission.

Is distribution an important economic function performed by the investment bank in its involvement as market maker in primary capital markets? Or would it be rational for the issuer to economise on the costs of distribution by having the investment bank certify the issue and then invite investors to apply directly to the firm for shares? After all, if distribution involves simply rationing shares in relation to excess demand between all who apply it is a simple clerical function which could be performed by anyone.

In this chapter it is argued that distribution by the investment bank provides a partial control of the adverse selection bias created by the presence of informed investors. It is demonstrated that investment banks can reduce the amount of under pricing required to compensate the uninformed for the adverse selection bias by rationing in a preferential manner to "regular clients" who behave as uninformed investors. Competition between investment banks assures that the most efficient distribution system survives in the market. This increases the expected revenue to the issuer.

The adverse selection model of the new issue market assumes than when an issue is over subscribed shares are rationed in relation to total demand among all investors. This model was used in chapter 2 to define the efficiency of new issue markets. However, it will be shown below that different methods of distribution imply different formulations of the "zero excess returns to the uninformed" efficiency condition. Therefore, efficiency must be measured relative to the method of distribution employed.

Having developed a theory of the role of distribution in determining efficiency we develop a method of testing this hypothesis by exploiting institutional and regulatory differences between new issue markets in the US and the UK. Specifically, the test is based on an assessment of the efficiency of the Placement new issue market in the UK and the initial public offering (IPO) new issue market in the US relative to the Offer for Sale new issue market in the UK. The reason for using the Offer for Sale as the benchmark for the test is that preferential allotments are prohibited for this method of making a new issue: Exchange regulations require that over subscribed shares be allotted among all investors in proportion to excess demand. Such restrictions do not apply to the Placement method in the UK or the IPO in the US. Therefore, it is expect that these markets are more efficient than the Offer for Sale new issue market.

The chapter is organised as follows: Section I reviews a model which explains how a system of distribution based on "bunching" controls a transactions difficulty—similar to that in new issue markets—created by the incentive of the buyer to sort for undervalued goods when pre-purchase quality information is expensive to produce—the specific example considered is the analysis of the De Beers' Central Selling Organisation. Section II develops the hypothesis that investment banks also have an incentive to develop a distribution system based on bunching to overcome the adverse selection bias against the lesser informed investors. Section III reviews alternative methods of making new issues in the UK and the US and specifies a test of the hypothesis that investment banks will choose a method of distribution which provides a partial offset to the adverse selection bias.

I.   The Economics of "Bunching" Selling Arrangements

Economists have recognised for some time that adverse selection biases can exist when pre-purchase quality information is costly to produce. In fact, a large branch of literature has developed to explain how institutional arrangements have evolved to overcome the transaction difficulties created by costly information. This literature has included reputation models and signalling models. This section examines how selling arrangements can be designed to overcome the transactions difficulties created by costly information. The example considered—the Central Selling Organisation of the De Beer's Group—involves "bunching" or average pricing to overcome the difficulty.

The Central Selling Organisation of the De Beers Group

The Central Selling Organisation of the De Beers' Group markets most of the world's gem-quality uncut diamonds. The essence of the selling arrangement is the following:

1.   The stones are sorted into categories with substantial variance in the value of stones within each category.
2.   Stones are sold to a small number of pre-selected buyers;
3.   The stones are sold in pre-selected blocks, called sights,.with the buyer specifying only the number of stones in the different categories which he wishes to buy.
4.   Buyers may inspect the sight before purchase but rejection results in the buyer's name being removed from the list of invited customers.

Barzel (1977) and Kenny and Klein (1983) suggest that the competitive advantage which assures the virtual monopoly position of the CSO in the wholesale diamond market is that it minimises buyer "oversearching" for quality information. In the absence of the CSO selling arrangement, it is argued, buyers would have the incentive to search for the stones which are undervalued at the average price chosen for stones in each group. The attempt by buyers to discover under priced stones would lead to lower total revenue being received by De Beers and increased expenditure on quality sorting by the CSO to produce more accurate pricing. The increased quality search by the CSO and by buyers would be duplicative and potentially wasteful because 1. the increased quality search of the CSO would be duplicated, perhaps more than once, by buyers and 2. because when the stone is being cut the cutter must again duplicate the quality inspection. The distributive gains from buyer oversearch thus result in a social waste of the resources devoted to this activity.

The fact that pre-purchase quality information is costly to produce results in "excessive quality search" and lower total revenue to the seller. The real resource costs resulting from an attempt to realise distributive gains because of "average pricing" are socially wasteful, in a zero transactions costs world, since there exists a transfer from one individual to another which will eliminate the incentive to engage in this distributive activity and thus reduce the resource cost of quality search. Such a transaction will leave both parties better off and result in a social gain. In line with this view Barzel argues that:

> The fact that many information situations have the potential for
> waste does not necessarily mean that waste occurs. If in the
> aggregate, these actions produce a negative product,
> arrangements that successfully restrain them or reduce their
> impact will generate a positive return (p. 292).

However, in assessing the desirability of eliminating buyer quality search one must take account of the potential social gains associated with this practice. If there are social gains associated with buyer quality search—that is the allocation of resources is improved—it will not in general pay to eliminate all of the incentive to engage in this sorting activity. Whether there is a social gain from a person examining the quality of goods they do not then purchase depends on the nature of the goods in question. If, within each quality category alternative units of a commodity are perfect substitutes for different buyers the social costs associated with eliminating buyer quality search are zero. Consequently, the net social gain from eliminating the incentive for buyer quality search is the real resource cost that buyers and sellers expend on duplicative inspections which produce only distributive gains for the buyer. The gain to the seller is the increased revenue it receives from sales **plus** savings on quality search **less** costs of enforcing pre-selection.

In the case of De Beers, Kenny and Klein argue that,

> Each wholesale buyer places essentially the same value on
> rough uncut stones offered for sale by De Beers.....Because
> wholesale search is not necessary for the stones to go to the
> highest valuing ultimate user, and because whoever purchases
> the stones must inspect each closely no matter how much pre-
> purchase inspection was done in the aggregate by other
> potential buyers, duplicate inspections waste real resources (p.
> 504).

The CSO discourages buyers from engaging in quality search by
pricing sights in such a way that buyers, on average, are earning rents,
the expected present value of which is greater, in almost all cases, than
the potential profit that can be achieved by the buyer rejecting sights of
lower than average quality. Since these rents are lost if the buyer rejects
the sight and is terminated from the CSO's list of invited buyers, a
wealth maximising buyer will not generally reject the sight. The CSO in
turn is prevented from reducing the average quality of the sights thus
making a short-term profit, by the return which it realises on its
reputation capital. If seller cheating is detected buyers will not continue
to participate in the pre-selection arrangement and the seller will loose
the stream of future rents arising from the scheme.

Finally, as Kenny and Klein note, the CSO could prevent buyer
quality sorting without giving any rents to buyers by merely prohibiting
buyer search; that is, the buyer pays before examining the sight.

> The problem involved in prohibiting all consumers pre-
> purchase inspections is that it creates an increased incentive for
> the seller to cheat buyers and hence requires a larger brand-
> name capital...Permitting pre-purchase inspections reduces the
> CSO's short-run cheating potential but as we have seen makes it
> necessary to share the marketing cost saving of the CSO selling
> arrangement with buyers to prevent rejection of the sight. For
> the CSO this is cheaper than the increased brand- name capital
> investment required under blindness (pp. 515- 16).

Essential Aspects of the Bunching System of Distribution

The essential features of the analysis of the potentially wasteful information situation which the De Beers' blockbooking or bunching system of distribution is designed to circumvent are the following:

1. The improvement in resource allocation (the social gain) arising from pre-purchase quality search is minimal—all wholesalers will place essentially the same value on an uncut diamond as they would each cut it in virtually the same manner given its structural characteristics.

2. Buyers are pre-selected and blockbooking or bunching is enforced—buyers rationally participate in this system of distribution because the net present value of the stream of rents which they earn is greater than the short-term gains from rejecting overvalued sights.

3. The incentive of the seller to expropriate the wealth of buyers by deliberately supplying lower than anticipated quality is controlled by the rents which the seller earns on invested reputation capital.

The parallel between the incentive of diamond buyers to engage in quality search and the incentive of investors to 'sort' between new issues seems clear—diamond buyers (investors) have an incentive to sort for undervalued diamonds (issues). In each case the sorting activity produces transactions difficulties which impose costs on the seller and which are costly to overcome. The adverse selection model examines how under pricing controls the transaction difficulties created by the dual problem of quality search and differential access to information. The remainder of this chapter examines how a system of distribution based on bunching reduces the cost of overcoming the transaction difficulty created by the uneven distribution of information in new issue markets.

II.   Bunching in the New Issue Market

A system of investor pre-selection or bunching, similar to the De Beers' CSO selling arrangement could, theoretically, operate to control the adverse selection bias in new issue markets. Following the analysis of Barzel (1977) and Kenny and Klein (1982) such a method of distributing new issues would increase the efficiency of the new issue market if:

1.   The improvement in resource and risk allocation (the social gain) resulting from investors' sorting for undervalued issues is minimal.

2.   Investors can be induced to participate in this bunching arrangement for the distribution of new issues by the receipt of rents on average.

3.   The reputation of the investment bank eliminates the incentive to perform in a manner other than that expected by investors— that is, the investment bank does not behave opportunistically.

Two alternative models of the distribution system in new issue markets are developed in this chapter. The first assumes a distribution system which provides a complete control of the adverse selection bias. The model assumes that there is a set of explicit contracts which rigidly enforce bunching. The aim is to specify a set of assumptions for which such a system of distribution is efficient. The second model assumes preferential allotments by investment banks to their regular clients who are determined to be uninformed. This system is shown to provide a partial solution to the adverse selection bias.

The models of the distribution system employed in this chapter are developments of the adverse selection model in chapter 2: that is, they embody all of the assumptions of the adverse selection model—and employ a similar notation—with the exception that a different method of distribution is employed.

Eliminating the Adverse Selection Bias by Bunching

The simplest model of distribution with bunching assumes that the investment bank adopts a system of Placement where investors are pre-selected— a group of N pre-selected identical investors each agree to purchase pZ/N of each issue. This commitment is made prior to the pricing of the issue. This system of distribution eliminates the adverse selection bias against these investors since the probability of allotment for all issues for these N investors is 1.

This section sets out a number of assumptions under which such a system of pre-selection or bunching provides an efficient solution to the adverse selection bias. The purpose of the analysis is not to contradict the explanation of under pricing in the adverse selection model but to illustrate the importance of the method of distribution in determining the relative efficiency of new issue markets. The remainder of this section examines the applicability of the bunching analysis of the De Beers'

CSO to the new issue markets. The parallel to each of the main elements of the De Beers analysis (discussed above) illustrates the incentive of the investment bank to ration in a preferential manner to uninformed investors:

1.   **The social gains from "investor quality search":** Portfolio theory makes the distinction between systematic or market related risk and unsystematic or diversifiable risk. Systematic risk refers to the risk which a security adds to a well diversified portfolio. This theory predicts that in competitive capital markets only mean expected return and systematic risk are relevant in determining share price. Furthermore securities will have close to perfect substitutes since the systematic risk characteristics of a particular security can be duplicated by a correctly chosen portfolio of other securities.

If 1. portfolio theory provides an adequate description of capital markets 2. the investments bank's estimate of share value is unbiased 3. the error in the bank's estimate is uncorrelated with market movements and 4. the investment bank incurs the socially optimum expenditure in valuing the issue—see below — the risk that a particular issue is mis-priced is diversifiable and therefore investors will not be compensated for taking this risk in competitive capital markets.

Under these assumptions the sorting between issues does not produce an improvement in the allocation of resources or risk—all investors are equally capable of diversifying risk and the investment bank has devoted the socially optimum amount of resources to determining the value of the issue. Pre-purchase quality search produces distributive gains only.

2.   **Rents to induce the participation of investors in the bunching system of distribution:** As in the De Beers example investors could be induced to participate in the pre-selection distribution arrangement if such participation secured an expected stream of rents the present value of which is greater than the short-term gains from rejecting an issue. The investment bank could potentially achieve this by under pricing on average and assuring allotments to these investors. Where d is the size of the discount required to secure the participation of investors each would receive an expected rent each period of $d(pZ/n)$. If all of the pre-selected investors were uninformed—

that is their expected gain from sorting was zero—the expected discount required to secure their participation would be close to zero. The larger the expected gain from sorting the greater are the required rents to secure the participation of investors.

In this simple model it is assumed that a sufficient discount is offered on average to secure the participation of the group of pre- selected investors in the bunching system of allotment. Thus under pricing represents a means of inducing investors to behave as uninformed.

3.   **Investment bank reputation:** As in the De Beers' example it is assumed that reputation ensures that the investment bank does not behave in a manner which exploits the   pre-selected investors—that is the investment bank produces an unbiased estimate of the value of each issue. It is possible for the investment bank to default on this commitment in one of two ways:

First: failing to conduct a sufficiently detailed analysis of the issuer in order to assess the value of the issue. This difficulty arises from the fact that the issuer has the incentive to search for an investment bank until it finds one which overvalues the firm. Therefore, a certain amount of expenditure by the investment bank on information production is required to control this incentive—otherwise the investment bank would be producing biased estimates of firm value with the implication of negative expected returns to the uninformed. An investment bank may have the incentive to economise on this expenditure in order to reduce costs or increase expected revenue—gain origination and distribution fees which it would otherwise not have obtained.

Second: deliberately overvaluing the issue in order to gain additional revenue from its initiation and distribution services. In essence this involves collusion between the issuer and the investment in order to exploit investors.

It is assumed that the incentive to behave in either of these ways is controlled by the stream of rents which the investment bank earns on its reputation capital. The definition of reputation most suitable in the context of investment banking is that suggested in Darby and Lott (1983). Darby and Lott define reputation as the source of the ability to charge a positive price for information. Reputation is built through the free provision of information since individuals will not generally pay for information from an unknown source—in their example quality information is provided free of charge by supplying higher quality output at the price of lower quality output. Thus reputation is established by a period of investment during which income is foregone. Once reputation is established the producer earns a stream of rents which cover the cost of the investment—entry assures that it is no higher. Thus, according to the approach of Darby and Lott, an investment bank could for example build a reputation in providing information to investors by engaging in security analysis and distributing it widely, free of charge.

The analysis in the section illustrates the incentive of investment banks to ration over subscribed issues in a preferential manner. Such a rationing scheme reduces the extent of the adverse selection bias and thus the amount of under pricing required to secure the participation of the uninformed. The next section presents some casual evidence that investment banks in the US do in fact adopt such a rationing scheme.

The Importance of the Method of Distributing New Issues

The purpose of the above discussion was not to contradict the explanation of under pricing in the adverse selection model but to emphasise the importance of distribution in determining the efficiency of new issue markets. Observation of the real world clearly shows that such a rigid system of investor pre-selection as described above does not exist: there are no explicit contract to enforce bunching in new issue markets. Equally, however, casual observation does suggest the importance of continuing relationships between investors and investment banks in determining allotments in heavily demanded issues.

Casual evidence from the US suggests that investment banks ration in a preferential manner to regular clients. A SEC study on the US new issue market documents evidence that investment banks and security dealers who retail to the public generally do so to small groups of customers "a hard core of customers whom they know well" (SEC 1963, p.523): "New issues are allotted to customers who are known to the principals of the firm and whose investment decisions were strongly influenced by their recommendations" (SEC 1963 p. 523).

There is also evidence that investment banks ration shares in new issues to investors who take a "long term view". This is again consistent with the hypothesis that investment banks chose a distribution system which favours the uninformed and reduces the returns to becoming informed. Investors who take a short term view apply simply because they believe that the investment bank has mis-priced the issue—these investors typically make large orders and trade on a margin account. It is reasonable to assume that the "long term investor" behaves more like the uninformed investor. "Most underwriters stated that in making allotments to customers they attempted to place the stock where long-term investment was likely" (SEC 1963 p. 523). The following quotation illustrates this point:

> People think that they can buy something today and sell it
> tomorrow but we do relatively little of that. Most of our
> customers, by far the biggest majority, are cash customers.
> They are generally investment clientele, varying from widows
> to businessmen that can afford to take a variety of merchandise
> and are interested in the variety of merchandise that comes
> along (SEC 1963 p. 523—Whiet, Weld & Co.).

Rationing in a preferential manner to regular clients produces a gain in efficiency if the rationing mechanism rewards those investors who are uninformed. Given the long term relationship between client and investment bank the bank is able to assess whether or not a particular investor is behaving as uninformed. It is argued below that rationing to regular clients who are uninformed produces a gain in efficiency.

It may also be argued that the structure and operation of the syndicate system in the US also reduces the potential gains to the uninformed and therefore the amount of under pricing required to compensate the uninformed. The discussion of the syndicate system is contained in section III of this chapter.

The alternative to the hypothesis that the system of preferential allotments and the syndicate system operates to increase the efficiency of the new issue market—by reducing the extent of the adverse selection bias against the uninformed—is that they enable the investment bank to exploit monopoly gains from its involvement in the new issue market. This alternative is discussed below.

The following section sets out a simple model in which investment banks ration in a preferential manner to regular clients who behave as uninformed investors. This method of distribution provides a partial control for the adverse selection bias against these investors.

Modelling the Preferential Allotments to Uninformed

The following assumptions are made regarding operation of the preferential rationing system adopted by investment banks:

1. The issuer conducts a test to determine whether or not each application is from an informed or uninformed investor on the basis of information on the past behaviour of the investor—both with new issues and other stock transactions. The probabilities of the different outcomes of this test are:

Probabilities associated with the test to determine investor type

	Result of test:	
Type of investor:	Informed	Uninformed
Informed	p_I	$(1 - p_I)$
Uninformed	$(1 - p_U)$	p_U

2. Each application which is determined to be from an informed investor is eliminated from the allotment procedure provided that the total demand from those investors who have been determined to be uninformed exceeds issue size—that is, over subscribed issues are allotted only to those investors who are believed to be uninformed.

3. Allotment of over subscribed issues, between those investors who have been determined to be uninformed, is by lottery: "uninformed" applications are drawn at random and completely filled until there are no more shares.

In addition to the above rationing scheme we make the following simplifying assumption before examining the probabilities of allotment in each state for the uninformed: given the realisation of demand the investment bank knows whether or not the informed have applied. Therefore, in the case where the informed have not applied—when the issue is overvalued—the investment bank does not apply the testing procedure to determine investor type: that is $p_u = 1$ when $v < p$.

Given the above distribution system the probabilities of allotment for the uninformed in the various states are:

$$b'_N = p\{\text{allotment in bad state}\}$$

$$= \min\left\{\frac{pZ}{NT}, 1\right\}$$

$$b_N = p\{\text{allotment in good state}\}$$

$$= p_N\left\{\frac{pZ}{p_N NT + (1 - p_I)I}, 1\right\}$$

Given this formulation it is a relatively simple matter to demonstrate that the equilibrium full subscription price is higher than in the model without preferential allotment to the uninformed provided that:

$$p_N > (1 - p_I) \tag{3.1}$$

That is, the equilibrium amount of under pricing is reduced when the sorting mechanism is efficient at determining whether or not an investor is uninformed.

At the full subscription offer price the adverse selection bias, assuming preferential rationing, b_N/b'_N, equals:

$$b_N/b'_N = \frac{pZ}{NT + [(1 - p_I)/p].I} \tag{3.2}$$

since at the full subscription price $b' = 1$. At the full subscription offer price for the model without preferential rationing the adverse selection bias, b/b', as derived in chapter 2, is:

$$b/b' = \frac{pZ}{NT+I}$$

It follows therefore that the extent of the adverse selection bias is less with preferential rationing, that is

$$b_N/b'_N > b/b' \tag{3.3}$$

if the condition concerning the efficiency of the preferential allotment procedure in (3.1) is met. Since the extent of the adverse selection bias is less with preferential rationing it follows, from the analysis of chapter

2, that the full subscription offer price is higher than in the case where all applicants have equal probability of allotment.

The Role of Under Pricing with Bunching

Under pricing in the new issue market with preferential allotments to uninformed investors serves two distinct functions:
1.   Compensation for any remaining adverse selection bias: under pricing compensates the uninformed for any remaining adverse selection bias which results from the participation of informed investors—that is, those informed who are not screened out by the investment bank.
2.   Inducement for investors to participate in the distribution system based on bunching: the preferential allotment of under priced issues to the uninformed investors is such that on average they earn rents, the expected present value of which are sufficient to induce them not to behave as informed investors.

III.   Institutional Arrangements in UK and US New Issue Markets

This section outlines the institutional arrangements in three new issue markets:
1.   Offer for Sale of the London Stock Exchange.
2.   Placement of the London Stock Exchange.
3.   IPO regulated by the SEC in the US.

The Offer for Sale

The Offer for Sale is the most commonly used method of making an initial public offering of equity by obtaining a full listing on the London Stock Exchange. Exchange regulations require that all firms above a certain minimum size use this method: the minimum size requirement is set quite low so that it affects about 75% of the firms making initial public offerings. The disclosure requirements of the Offer for Sale are as stringent as US standards: for example the company must produce at least five years of audited accounts, produce a full account of directors interests and principal contracts, make a statement about the use of funds, etc. In addition it must ensure wide distribution of its offering prospectus by publishing it in full in at least two national daily newspapers.

The principal feature of the Offer for Sale which distinguishes it from other methods of making new issues is that the Stock Exchange regulates the method of distribution of shares. Specifically, it requires that over subscribed issues be allotted in proportion to the degree of over subscription between all investors: the basis of allotment is for large applications to be scaled down in relation to the degree of over subscription while smaller applications are selected by ballot for allotment in full or on a partially scaled down basis out of a pool which reflects the size of these orders in relation to total demand (London Stock Exchange 1985). This method of allotment is equivalent in a probability sense to the rationing scheme assumed in the adverse selection model (see chapter 4 section II). The Stock Exchange requires that the demand for the issue be published as a way of policing the allotment procedures for the issue. The Stock Exchange operates this system with the motivation of achieving as wide a distribution of the shares as possible.

Because of the equivalence between the method of allotment of the adverse selection model and the Offer for Sale this method of making an initial public offering presents an ideal opportunity to test the adverse selection model and the efficiency of the new issue market as defined by the model. The Offer for Sale also provides a useful benchmark for assessing the importance of the method of distribution in determining the relative efficiency of new issue markets.

The Placement of the London Stock Exchange

The Placement is the second most commonly used method of making an initial public offering of equity by obtaining a listing on the London Stock Exchange. The Placement in the UK is significantly different from a Placement which, in the context of an initial equity offering, is a distribution to a small number of chosen investors with no after market developing in the shares. The Placement of the London Stock Exchange has more is common with the IPO in the US than with a Placement: the shares are distributed widely and an active after market develops so that price quotations are widely available.

Only companies below a certain minimum size requirement are permitted to use the Placement method as a means of achieving a full listing on the London Stock Exchange. The disclosure requirements of the Placement are almost identical to those of the Offer for Sale—five years of audited accounts are also required. The company is also required to assure wide availability of its prospectus although it need publish it only in one national daily newspaper.

The principal difference between the Offer for Sale and the Placement is that the method of distribution is not as highly regulated by the Stock Exchange. The investment bank has discretion in determining the allotment procedure of over subscribed shares: that is, the investment bank can ration in a preferential manner to its regular clients.

The IPO in the US

The main distinguishing feature of the Initial Public Offering in the US is the operation of the syndicate system for underwriting and distribution. In the UK syndicates are formed only to underwrite the issue: the underwriting group—or sub-underwriters as they are known in the UK—does not participate in the distribution of the issue. However, in the US the syndicate pays an important role in distribution. Initiation, the process of determining the structure and pricing of the issue, is performed by a single investment bank—the initiating investment bank (IIB).

The syndicate of investment banks and security dealers formed by the initiating investment bank to underwrite and distribute the issue can be divided into two distinct groups:

1. The Purchase Group: the function of the purchase group is to underwrite the issue. The group consists of a small number of investment banks who each agree to purchase a fixed proportion of the issue at a fixed concession—negotiated by the IIB—below the public offering price. For a 2% spread— difference between public offering price and the price paid to the issuer—the purchase group would typically receive 0.75%. Any unsold shares and expenses associated with stabilisation during the syndication period are allotted between the participants of the group in relation to the size of their participation. The group is governed by the purchase group agreement, also known as the agreement among underwriters, which is distinct from the underwriting agreement which is between the IIB, on behalf of the group, and the issuing company.

2. The Selling Group: the selling group, whose function it is distribution, consists of a larger number of investment banks

and security dealers. The selling group includes members of the purchase group but also includes other investment banks and varies in number with the size of the issue—it sometimes includes several hundred firms. The group is governed by the selling group agreement, also called the selective dealer agreement, which sets forth the terms of the agreement, establishes the size of the selling concession—usually half of the gross concession—and provides of the termination of the group, usually within 30 days.

The purchase group agreement appoints the syndicate manager as agent for the purchase group in negotiating with the company and signing the underwriting agreement. As such it authorises the manager to determine the time of the initial offering and the offer price. The agreement also restricts members from selling below the public offering price—although there are some exception for sales to syndicate members and members of the National Association of Security Dealers. During the life of the agreement the public offering price and the concession to dealers may be changed only by the syndicate manager.

The purchase group and selling group are formed and the agreements signed prior to the determination of the offer price. Nevertheless, a members may withdraw at any point up to the time of the final determination of the offer price and the signing of the underwriting agreement with the issuing firm. However, cancellation seldom occurs. Such behaviour is almost assuredly accompanied by the absence of further invitations to join syndicates managed by that, and possibly other, investment banks. Furthermore, investment banks who participate successfully in the syndicate of one lead manager are generally included in other syndicates of the same manager. That is, a system of "bunching" is applied to the formation of syndicates to underwrite and distribute the issue.

Evidence presented at the investment bank anti-trust trial, which lasted from 1949 to 1953, demonstrated such continuing relationships between investment banks in determining the structure of syndicates. For example, from the testimony of Mr Stuart, who was described by Judge Medina as a man "whose testimony I could rely on with confidence [and] ..... who broke the case for the Government" (Carosso 1970 pp. 491-2):

Because the originating banker needed to maintain good relations with other firms on whom he could call more or less continuously, he naturally tried to keep fellow underwriters and distributors happy. One way to do this was to invite successive participations by those whose performance was satisfactory (U.S. vs Morgan p. 14346).

Such syndicate based relationships between investment banks and security dealers can be rationalised by the version of the adverse selection model developed in this chapter. Investment banks has an incentive to ration in a preferential manner to those who behave as uninformed investors. Similar incentives exist for the IIB in determining participations in the syndicate system of underwriting and distribution. To illustrate this point we examine how selective participation by firms in syndicates affects the efficiency of the new issue market:

1.   Selective participation in the purchase group and the efficiency of underwriting markets: if some firms participate in the underwriting syndicate on a selective basis they will increase the expected losses for the lead underwriter, the IIB, and those who do not participate on a selected basis. This is the case even if those who participate selectively do not have as much information the IIB—this point may be demonstrated in a similar manner to the model developed in the Appendix to chapter 2. With selective participation therefore the size of the equilibrium concession required to yield a zero expected return to the IIB from underwriting would be increased.

2.   Selective participation in the selling group and the efficiency of the distribution system: assume that individual members of the selling group operate a preferential allotment system, of the type described in section II, to their regular clients. Suppose, however, that members of the selling group can participate selectively having observed the offer price set by the IIB. They will participate in issues which they believe have been undervalued. In this case the preferential rationing scheme operated by each firm will assure positive expected returns to their clients which can be recouped in the form of higher than competitive charges for its services. This pattern of participation by some firms will result in negative expected returns to the investors of those firms who participate in all issues—requiring a higher equilibrium level of under pricing—

and may also increase the expected losses from underwriting and thus the required underwriting concession.

The above discussion illustrates the rationale for prohibiting selective participation in the purchase group and selling group from the perspective of the adverse selection model developed in this chapter.

Testing the Importance of Distribution

Because of the institutional and regulatory differences between the new issue markets examined above it is possible to devise a test of the role of distribution in determining market efficiency. The test of the hypothesis is as follows:

1. Offer for Sale (UK): the least efficient because the investment bank is prohibited from rationing shares in a preferential manner.

2. Placement (UK): more efficient than the Offer for Sale because the investment bank has discretion to determine the method of allotment.

3. IPO (US): more efficient than the Offer for Sale because preferential allotments are possible and, also, more efficient that the Placement because the syndication distribution system is more highly developed in the US.

Loosely speaking, one new issue market is more efficient than another if there is less under pricing in that market. However, it is not sufficient to look only at the average amount of under pricing in each market because average uncertainty differs between these markets:

1. Firms above the Stock Exchange's minimum size requirement are required to use the Offer for Sale—smaller—more difficult to value firms use the Placement;

2. The Stock Exchange requires companies to produce 5 years of audited accounts if they are to obtain a full listing on the Exchange. This applies to the Offer for Sale and the Placement. In the US start- up ventures may make an initial public offering provided that they meet the SEC's regulatory requirements.

Therefore, the test of relative efficiency used is to estimate the uncertainty-under pricing trade-off in each market. One market is defined as being more efficient than another if for a given increase in uncertainty there is a smaller increase in the expected amount of under pricing. The methodology for estimating the uncertainty-under pricing trade-off is discussed in detail in chapter 5. The results of the test provide strong support for the hypothesis that the method of distribution of new issues has an important bearing on the relative efficiency of these markets.

The alternative hypothesis is that the distribution system employed by investment banks is used to extort monopsony profits from the new issue market: Investment banks ration in a preferential manner to regular clients who remit side payments in the form of higher than competitive charges on other services. The implication of this hypothesis is that the relationship between under pricing and uncertainty should be more unfavourable in markets where the investment bank has discretion in determining the method of allotment: under pricing would have to compensate the investor for the expected value of the adverse selection bias and the higher than competitive charges on the other services provided by the bank.

Chapter 4

Testing the Efficiency of
New Issue Markets

Introduction

The apparent under pricing of initial equity offerings was once considered prima facia evidence of the inefficiency of new issue markets. However, the adverse selection model of new issue markets, developed by Rock (1982 & 1986), suggests that under pricing may be an efficient response to a bias in the probability of allotment between undervalued and overvalued issues against uninformed investors because of the participation of a group of informed investors. Current thinking is, therefore, that the appropriate test of the efficiency of new issue markets is to test the competitive equilibrium predicted by the adverse selection model.

This chapter provides a direct test of the competitive equilibrium predicted by the adverse selection model by using a sample of issues conducted by the Offer for Sale in the UK. This sample presents an ideal opportunity to test the adverse selection model because realised demand for these issues becomes public information and also because the method of allotment for over subscribed issues, which is regulated by the London Stock Exchange, is similar to that assumed by the adverse selection model.

The chapter is organised as follows: Section I outlines the tests conducted. Section II introduces the sample used and examines some preliminary evidence on under pricing from the UK. Section III tests the equilibrium condition of zero expected returns for the uninformed.

Section IV tests the equilibrium condition of zero expected return for underwriting.

I.   Testing the Efficiency of New Issue Markets

The only existing explanation of under pricing consistent with efficient capital markets is the adverse selection model. Therefore, testing the equilibrium conditions of this model amounts to a test of new issue market efficiency as understood in current literature. However, the only test of the hypothesis conducted to date is a test for the positive relationship between initial returns and measures of the ex ante uncertainty predicted by the model (see Beatty (1984), Beatty and Ritter (1986) and chapter 1 section II). However, this is not a conclusive test of the adverse selection model since the existence of such a relationship is also predicted by the main alternative hypothesis—the monopoly power hypothesis (see chapter 2 section IV).

The most conclusive test of the adverse selection model of the new issue market is to explicitly test the equilibrium conditions of the model as developed in chapter 2.

Zero Expected Returns to Uninformed Investors

An implication of the adverse selection model of investor behaviour is that the expected return to the uninformed investor is zero. This equilibrium condition is an implication of the risk neutrality assumption, rational expectations and competition between the uninformed to obtain shares in the new issue—the model in chapter assumes a constant level of informed wealth Since this equilibrium holds for all levels of informed demand it generalises to the case where the number of informed investors is endogenously determined, assuming that discounting remains rational for the issuer (see Rock 1982 chapter 2).

It is important to stress that this equilibrium condition is an implication of the rational and competitive behaviour by investors and that it holds independently of the behaviour of the issuer/investment bank. That is, competition between investors will assure zero expected return for the uninformed even if the issuer/investment bank under prices more than predicted by the competitive model.

It is therefore, necessary to specify an independent test to determine whether the issuer/investment bank sets the offer price in the manner predicted by the adverse selection model. The test conducted in this chapter is to estimate the expected return to underwriters.

Zero Expected Returns from Underwriting

The analysis of the pricing decision of the issuer in chapter 2 suggests that, where discounting is rational, the issuer sets the offer price at the full subscription price—that is, the price at which the level of uninformed demand equals issue size. However, this conclusion may not be implemented as a testable implication of the competitive behaviour of the issuer/investment bank as the specification of the model on which the conclusion assumes that uninformed demand is non-stochastic: As discussed in chapter 2, with stochastic uninformed demand it may be rational for the issuer/investment bank to set the offer price such that expected uninformed demand is larger than issue size. Even in this case the expected revenue from the issue is less than issue size because realised revenue can never be larger than, but can be less than, issue size.

Thus, while the adverse selection model with non-stochastic uninformed demand predicts that in equilibrium:

Uninformed demand = Issue Size = Total Revenue

the model, generalised to the case of stochastic uninformed demand, suggests that:

Expected Uninformed Demand > Issue Size > Expected Total Revenue

However, it is possible to derive an alternative implication of the efficient behaviour of the issuer/investment bank, predicted by a more general specification of the adverse selection model, by examining the expected returns to underwriters. It was argued that with stochastic uninformed demand the underwriter must be compensated for the shortfall of expected revenue below to issue size. Assuming risk neutrality, the equilibrium expected return to the underwriter is zero if the investment bank sets the offer price at the level predicted by the competitive adverse selection model.

The alternative hypothesis, that under pricing results from investment banks exploiting the inexperience of the issuers, predicts that the expected return to underwriters will be positive because of:

1.   "Excessive" under pricing to increase the size of expected uninformed demand and thus expected revenue from the issue.

2.   Higher than competitive underwriting concessions.

To conclude, therefore, the first test demonstrates that the uninformed are compensated for the adverse selection bias and that investors behave as predicted by the competitive adverse selection model. The second represents a test of the equilibrium behaviour of the issuer/investment bank predicted by the model.

Testing Efficiency of the Offer for Sale

Rock (1986 p. 205) also concludes that "the crucial test of the model involves observing the degree to which shares are rationed on the offer date. If the model is correct, weighing the returns by the probabilities of obtaining an allotment should leave the uninformed investor earning the riskless rate"—this is strictly true only when the uninformed are risk neutral. The difficulty with conducting such a test is that the extent and nature of rationing is not made public information. It is generally argued, for instance Rock (1986. p 205), that investment banks do not reveal information of the level of demand since this reflects on its performance in pricing the issue and because of frequent complaints that shares are rationed to regular clients on a preferential basis (see chapter 3 section III).

The test of the equilibrium conditions of the adverse selection model is based on a database of offers for sale, onto the London Stock Exchange, for which information on the demand for each issue and the method of allotment is public information. The database was obtained from Singer & Friedlander (various issues).

Stock Exchange regulations require that over subscribed issues be allotted in proportion to the degree of over subscription: the basis of allotment is for large applications to be scaled down in relation to the degree of over subscription while smaller applications are selected by ballot for allotment in full or on a partially scaled down basis out of a pool which reflects the size of these orders in relation to total demand (London Stock Exchange 1985). This method of allotment is equivalent, in a probability sense, to the rationing scheme assumed in the adverse selection model (see section III of this chapter).

Therefore it is possible to directly test the efficiency of the Offer for Sale new issue market against the equilibrium conditions of the adverse selection model developed in chapter 2. The equilibrium conditions of the adverse selection model must be adapted if a different method of distribution is employed. For example, if a more efficient method of distribution were employed (see Chapter 3) the measures of expected return based on the adverse selection model in chapter 2 would imply negative returns to the uninformed.

Stock Exchange regulations require information on the demand for each issue to be published. This provides investors a with a way of assessing whether they received a "fair" allotment and is thus a way of policing the required rationing procedure for over subscribed issues.

II.   Evidence on Under Pricing from the UK

During the 10 year period 1971-80, 241 companies conducted successful initial public offerings of common stock by means of the Offer for Sale. The sample used in this study includes all of these issues with the exception of 3 issues for which information on the demand for each issue was unavailable. The measure of demand used is termed "number of times subscribed" and is defined as total demand divided by issue size. For each of these 238 offers in the 1971-80 period an initial return relative to the offer price was calculated using the last trade price on the first day of trading and equivalently for the first month of trading, IR_1 and IR_m respectively. The initial return measures were also adjusted for market movements between the date of publication of the prospectus and the end of the first day and month of trading, AIR_1 and AIR_m. In the UK the prospectus is published and the offer price set about two weeks before trading in the share can commence on the Stock Exchange.

The Distribution of Initial Returns in the UK

The distribution of first day returns adjusted for market movements, AIR_1, for the 238 offers in this sample is presented in figure 4.1. This distribution has many characteristics in common with studies of initial returns conducted for US new issues (see chapter 1). Specifically, the distribution exhibits a statistically significant positive mean initial return of 7.43% with large standard deviation of 15.6% and is positively skewed. AIR_1 is positive in 156, or 65.5% of the cases. A t-test (see chapter 2 note 2) suggests that we accept the hypothesis that the investor has a better than even chance of randomly drawing an issue which experiences positive initial returns.

Average under pricing of 7.43% for the Offer for Sale is significantly less than the average for IPOs in the US—there the average is 18.8% (see Ritter 1984). This does not suggest, however, that UK new issue markets are more efficient than their counterparts in the US since the average uncertainty surrounding UK new issues is arguable less than in the US. Only relatively established companies (those with 5 years audited accounts and above a certain size—the smaller companies use the Placement) use the Offer for Sale while even start-up ventures or those with relatively short trading history come to market through the IPO. The assessment of relative efficiency must therefore be based on the analysis of the uncertainty- under pricing trade-off in section V.

The Demand Function for New Issues

The unique feature of this sample of new issues is the inclusion of information on the demand for each issue. Two features about this series of observations are immediately evident. Firstly, the variability of demand across issues is large: the standard deviation of the number of times subscribed is 21.5 times. Secondly, there is a close association between initial performance and the number of times subscribed. Figure 4.2 illustrates these points by presenting a scatter diagram of the relationship between initial returns and the number of times subscribed for the 238 offers in the sample. The following regression results summarise this relationship

$$\text{AIR} = -0.03 + 0.03\ln.d + 0.01(\ln.d)^2$$
$$\phantom{\text{AIR} =} (-3.41) \quad (6.04) \qquad (4.94) \qquad\qquad (4.1)$$

$$\bar{R}^2 = 58.3\%$$

where d is the number of times subscribed (t-statistics in parentheses— all parameters significant at the 1% level).

This relationship between initial performance and demand suggests that the demand curve for new issues is negatively sloped. This is consistent with the adverse selection formulation of the new issues market: Unsophisticated, or informed investors, apply for all issues, or apply randomly with respect to initial performance. Sophisticated, or informed investors, base the size of their application on an assessment of the value of the issue. If all investors were unsophisticated we would expect no relationship to exist between initial performance and the demand for the issue. Therefore, the negatively sloped demand function for new issues is evidence that some investors have an ability to "sort" for those which will have positive initial performance. This is sufficient to create an adverse selection bias against the uninformed.

The Relative Magnitude of Informed and Uninformed Demand

In this section we present evidence on the relative magnitude of informed and uninformed demand. The estimates are based on the assumption that uninformed demand, while stochastic, is independent of initial performance—the validity of this assumption is suggested by the following regression:

$$AIR(IR<0)_1 = -0.06 + 0.01 \ln.d_U + 0.00(\ln.d_U)^2$$
$$(-6.68) \quad (0.95) \qquad (0.36) \qquad\qquad (4.2)$$

$$\bar{R}^2 = 0.0\%$$

Where $AIR(IR<0)_1$ is the initial return for issues with negative returns and d_U is the demand for issues with negative returns—that is, uninformed demand.

In this case an unbiased estimate of uninformed demand can be derived by considering only those issues with negative initial returns: that estimated uninformed demand is average demand for the issues with negative initial returns—the issues for which the informed do not apply. Informed demand is estimated as average total demand for issues with positive initial returns less the estimate of average uninformed demand. The analysis shows that average uninformed demand is on average about 1.5 times issue size while informed demand is about 8 times issue size (see Table 4.1).

The evidence suggests that the investment bank sets the offer price to induce an average level of uninformed demand greater than issue size. This conclusion is consistent with the following hypotheses:
1.   Monopoly pricing by the investment bank: the investment bank under prices "excessively" in order to reduce distribution effort increase the expected revenue from the issue, and decrease underwriting losses.
2.   Efficient new issue pricing with stochastic uninformed demand as discussed in chapter 2.

The test of the expected returns to underwriters distinguishes between these alternative hypotheses.

The Risk Neutrality Assumption

The principal justification for the risk neutrality assumption made in chapter 2 is that initial returns are weakly related to movements in the market index. That is, provided that the investor is compensated for the expected losses caused by adverse selection the risks of uncertain initial returns can be controlled by diversification. In competitive markets agents will not be compensated for taking this risk—they will only be compensated for the expected value of losses arising from the adverse selection bias. Thus, though investors may require compensation for systematic risk, they can be viewed as behaving as if they were risk neutral with respect to the losses caused by issues which are mis-priced.

A test of the validity of this assumption is to estimate the relationship between initial returns and movements in the market index using the following regression model:

$$IR_1 = 0.07 + 1.13\,RM_1 \qquad\qquad (4.3)$$
$$(7.29) \quad (3.48)$$

$$\bar{R}^2 = 4.50\%$$

where RM_1 is the return on the market index from the date of the publication of the prospectus to the close of the first day of trading. The relationship illustrates that only a small proportion of total initial returns are explained by movements in the market and thus supports the justification of the risk neutrality assumption. The relationship for overvalued issues is:

$$IR(IR<0)_1 = -0.08 + 0.52\,RM_1 \qquad\qquad (4.4)$$
$$\phantom{IR(IR<0)_1 = }(9.92) \quad (3.01)$$

$$\bar{R}^2 = 12.2\%$$

This presents further justification for the risk neutrality assumption from the perspective of underwriters.

III.   The Expected Returns for the Uninformed Investor

The close correlation between initial performance and new issue demand provides strong support for proposition that informed investors participate in new issues markets. However, given 1. the method of allotment employed in the Offer for Sale and 2. information on the demand for each issue; it is possible to specify a more stringent test of the adverse selection model based on the equilibrium condition of zero expected return for uninformed investors.

Estimating Expected Return for the Uninformed

The estimate of the expected return for the uninformed is based on the fact that an equivalence, in the expected value sense, can be drawn between the Offer for Sale method of rationing shares and that assumed in the formal modelling of the adverse selection bias. Given this equivalence the observation on the number of times subscribed can be interpreted as an ex post measure of the probability of receiving an allotment in a new issue. The lottery rationing mechanism results in a probability of receiving an allotment of:

$$P\{\text{Allotment}\} = \min\left\{\frac{\text{issue size}}{\text{demand for issue}}, 1\right\}$$

(see chapter 2) which is exactly equivalent to the proportion of the subscription which an investor will have filled in an Offer for Sale where rationing is in proportion to excess demand—that is the probability of allotment with the lottery is the same as the proportion allotted where rationing is in proportion to excess demand.

For ease of exposition, in what follows it will be assumed that it is the lottery method of rationing which is employed in the Offer for Sale so that the probability interpretation of rationing can be applied. It follows, therefore, that an ex post measure of the probability of receiving an allotment can be obtained from the observation of the number of times an offer is subscribed, d, as follows

$$\tilde{P}\{\text{Allotment}\} = \min\left[\frac{1}{d}, 1\right] \tag{4.5}$$

Using this *ex-post* measure of the probability of allotment it is possible to estimate the expected return for an uninformed investor by taking an average over the sample of issues in the study as follows:

$$\tilde{E}_U[\text{gain}] = \sum_{i=1}^{n} w_i b_i IR_i \qquad (4.6)$$

where uninformed demand for each issue w_i is related to firm size (offer price by the total number of shares issued and held by the initial owners) adjusted for inflation.

Testing for Zero Expected Returns for the Uninformed

Table 4.2 contains the estimated value of the expected gain to the uninformed investor from new issue subscription for various measures of initial return and assuming that uninformed investors apply for all issues in relation to real firm size. The estimated expected first day initial return for the uninformed investor, taking account of the probability of allotment, is 0.08% as against a simple average initial return of 7.43%. The standard deviation of the initial performance adjusted for the probability of allotment is 4.3%. The distribution is presented as figure 4.3—its highly peaked nature about zero is further confirmation of the proposition that the expected return to a financially unsophisticated investor is zero.

The estimated expected return to the uninformed over the first month is 1.10%. This too provides strong support for the adverse selection hypothesis. The monthly average return of 1.10% implies an annual compound rate of return on unseasoned equity of 14.03% over the period 1971 to 1980. This is in line with the average return on the market index for this period.

Interpreting the Zero Expected Return Equilibrium

This test illustrates that the uninformed are compensated for the expected losses imposed by the adverse selection bias. The finding of zero expected returns to the uninformed is consistent with the competitive behaviour of investors described by the model in chapter 2. This is the strongest evidence offered to date supporting the adverse selection formulation of the new issue market.

Were investors to realise any gains from sorting using information on the valuation of the issue their expected return would be greater than zero.

It is important to reiterate that this test is a test of the demand side of the adverse selection model only. This equilibrium can hold independently of the behaviour of the issuer/investment bank. Even if the issuer/investment bank under prices by more than predicted by the competitive model—because, for example, the investment bank is exploiting the inexperience of the issuer—the competitive behaviour of investors can assure a zero expected return for the uninformed. Thus it is necessary to develop a second independent test to examine the efficiency of the pricing decision of the issuer/investment bank.

It was argued in chapter 2 section 4 that the test of zero expected returns to the underwriter provides such an independent test.

IV.   Efficient Underwriting Markets

It was argued in chapter 2 that, with efficient underwriting markets, the adverse selection model predicts that the expected return to the underwriter is zero. This conclusion, which is again dependent on the assumption risk neutrality, enables an indirect test of the proposition that the issuer/investment bank sets the offer price at the efficient level to overcome the adverse selection bias and that under pricing is not a reflection of the exploitation of the issuer. The test of efficient underwriting markets is conducted as follows:
1.   Estimate the size of the expected losses from underwriting.
2.   Estimate the size of the underwriting concession.
3.   Conduct a significance test of the difference between these estimates.

Estimating the Expected Cost of Under Subscription

An ex post measure of the expected losses from underwriting is obtained in the following manner: Define:

$$s_i = \max\{0, 1 - d_i\}$$
$$= 0 \iff d_i > 1$$
$$> 0 \iff d_i < 1$$

where s_i is the proportion the issue left with the underwriter and di is the number of times demand exceeds issue size. It is assumed that any unsold shares are sold in the after market at the ruling price v_i per share. In the absence of the concession the total loss to the investment bank from issue i is :

$$s_i Z_i(p_i - v_i) = [\text{no. shares sold below p}] \times [\text{loss per share}]$$

The percentage loss per share is given by siIRi. The average of the percentage loss per share for all of the issues in the sample provides an estimate of the expected loss per share from underwriting, denoted $\tilde{E}_I[\text{loss}]$

$$\tilde{E}_I[\text{loss per share}] = \sum_{i=1}^{n} s_i IR_i \qquad (4.7)$$

The Size of the Underwriting Concession

The database used in this study does not include an observation on the size of the underwriting concession received for each issue. However, information on the average size of the underwriting concession for the Offer for Sale is available from other studies. Dimson (1979 pp. 197-98) argues that the average size of the underwriting concession is in the region of 1.25%. This conclusion is also supported by Marsh (1980) and Briston and Herbert (1972). Since we do not have direct observations on the size of the underwriting concession for each issue it is necessary to base the test of competitive underwriting on the (unweighted) average derived in the above studies: that is we assume an average underwriting concession of 1.25%.

The estimate of the expected loss from under subscription is not weighted by issue size since the estimates of the size of the underwriting concession is based on an unweighted average.

Testing for Zero Expected Returns for Underwriters

Table 4.4 contains the estimated value of the expected loss per share from underwriting assuming that the underwriter sells any unsold shares at the price ruling in the market at the end of the first day and month of trading.

The results of the test of the difference of the estimated expected loss per share from the estimated concession per share, 1.25%, provide support for the hypothesis of competitive underwriting. The unweighted average expected underwriting loss over the first day of trading is 1.10% which is insignificantly different from 1.25%. The estimated underwriting loss over the first month is 1.03%—that this is smaller than the estimated loss over the first day is again consistent with the hypothesis that the underwriter is compensated for systematic over this period like any other investor. Table 4.3 presents the smallest significance level at which the null hypothesis would be rejected.

The tests of the equilibrium conditions of zero expected returns to uninformed investors and underwriters provides the strongest evidence to date concerning 1. the validity of the adverse selection hypothesis of under pricing and 2. the efficiency of new issue markets.

However, as discussed in chapter 3, the finding that the UK Offer for Sale new issue market is efficient should be interpreted as a finding of efficiency "given the particular method of distribution required by the Offer for Sale". The finding should not be interpreted a suggesting an absolute level of efficiency since alternative methods of distribution may provide a partial control for the adverse selection bias and require a "smaller amount of under pricing". In order to test the hypothesis that alternative methods of distribution provide a partial control for the adverse selection bias in new issue markets it is proposed to estimate the uncertainty-under pricing trade-off for the Offer for Sale and the Placement in the UK and the IPO in the US. these issues are examined in the following chapter.

Figure 4.1 Distribution of Adjusted Initial Returns for 238 Offers for Sale during 1971-80

Interval mean   Number of observations

Interval mean	N	
-.400	1	*
-.375		
-.350		
-.325		
-.300		
-.275		
-.250		
-.225		
-.200	1	*
-.175	1	*
-.150	2	**
-.125	8	********
-.100	10	**********
-.075	8	********
-.050	16	****************
-.025	23	***********************
.000	22	**********************.......................
.025	20	******************** frequency
.050	25	*************************
.075	18	******************
.100	13	*************
.125	14	**************
.150	8	********
.175	5	*****
.200	7	*******
.225	4	****
.250	3	***
.275	2	**
.300	5	*****
.325	6	******
.350	3	***
.375	2	**
.400	1	*
.425	1	*
.450		
.475	2	**
.500	2	**
.525	1	*
.550	1	*
.575	1	*
.600		
.625		
.650	1	*
.675		
.700	1	*

Note: First day initial returns adjusted for market movements between the date of the publication of the prospectus and the end of the first day's trading. * equals one observation.

Figure 4.2   **Scatter Diagram of Initial Returns vs Number of Times Subscribed**

AIR$_1$

```
0.9+
  -                              |
  -                              |
  -                              |
  -                              |              1
0.6+                             |                 1
  -                              |                 1   1 1
  -                              |                2 11
  -                              |                  2
  -                              |               12  12
0.3+                             |             1 2 12 121 11
  -                           |  1      1   1 11  1 1 1
  -                          | 1     11   1 2 211 121
  -                          |  12   212 162121322 2
  -                      1   4431 1225314133113 411
0.0+   ————————————2-33-122935134231231-1-1-1-1-1————
  -              2 122 23 4  53 12  21         1
  -        1     11 23 31 11 |112 1    1
  -                  1    |
  -                       |
-0.3+                      |
  -                       |
  -                       |      1
  -                       |
  -                       |
-0.6+                      |
      ————————+————————+————————+————————+————————+——
           -2.0     0.0     2.0     4.0     6.0
                  Ln No. Times Subscribed
        under subscribed ←|→ over subscribed
```

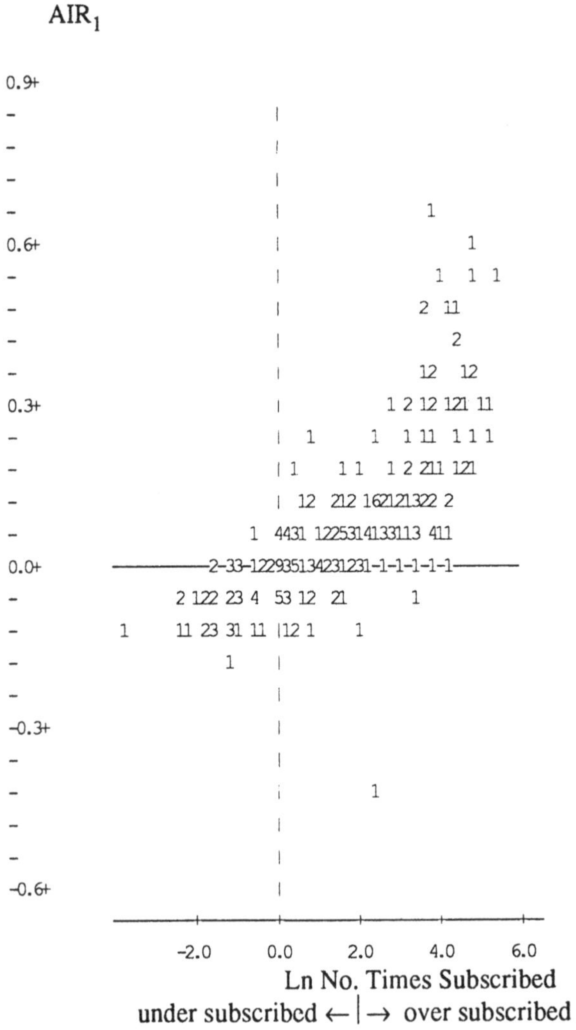

Note: Adjusted initial returns on the first day of trading vs the log of the number of times subscribed. The scatter diagram supports the finding of the non-linear relationship reported in the regression model above. 1-9 indicate the number of observations coincident on each point. At ln.d=0.0 d=1 that is, demand equals issue size.

Figure 4.3   Distribution of Adjusted Initial Returns for 238 Offers for Sale During 1971-80 Weighted by the Probability of Receiving Allotment

Interval mean		Number of observations
-.250		
-.225		
-.200	1	*
-.175	1	*
-.150	1	*
-.125	8	**
-.100	10	**
-.075	7	**
-.050	14	***
-.025	22	*****
.000	133	**************************------
.025	28	***** frequency
.050	8	**
.075	4	*
.100	1	*
.125		
.150	1	*
.175		
.200		

Note: First day initial returns adjusted for market movements between the date of the publication of the prospectus and the end of the first day's trading. * equals multiples of 1 to 5 observations. Probability of receiving allotment defined as min[1/(number of times subscribed), 1].

Table 4.1   Average Uninformed and Informed Demand

	Uninformed Demand (IR<0)		Total Demand (0>IR>0)		Informed Demand
	All Issues	Excluding Outliers	All Issues	Excluding Outliers	Excluding Outliers
IR_1	2.16 (3.86) [67]	0.90 (1.10) [63]	14.00 (24.84) [171]	9.31 (11.53) [145]	8.41
AIR_1	2.25 (5.93) [82]	1.77 (2.58) [80]	14.88 (24.84) [156]	10.02 (11.76) [131]	8.25
IR_m	2.34 (6.85) [74]	1.49 (2.03) [70]	13.49 (23.81) [164]	9.11 (11.38) [139]	7.62
AIR_m	2.45 (6.77) [88]	1.43 (2.02) [82]	14.64 (24.67) [150]	9.85 (11.59) [125]	7.37

Note: The measure of demand used is average constant price demand divided by average constant price issue size. The average is calculated for positive and negative initial returns weighing demand by real issue size. We calculate the size of informed and uninformed demand by eliminating outliers from the sample—outliers are defined as those observations for which excess demand lies outside 2 standard deviations of the mean.

One qualification must be added to these estimates of informed and uninformed demand. The estimates are based on the assumption that those investors with superior information—or ability to estimate after market initial performance such as institutional or professional investors—never mis-assess the value of the issue and apply for issues which will realise negative initial returns. This possibility was considered in the specification of the adverse selection model considered in chapter 3. The above estimate of uninformed demand is biased up if the informed do in fact make errors and apply for issues which in fact experience negative initial returns.

Standard deviation and number of issues in parentheses. Average demand defined as excess demand weighted by issue size (in constant prices). Outliers defined as issues for which excess demand is more than two standard deviations from the mean for the group.

Table 4.2   **Mean Initial Return and Initial Return Weighted by the Probability of Receiving an Allotment**

	IR_1	AIR_1	IR_m	AIR_m
Mean initial return	7.66%	7.43%	11.01%	9.87%
	(.000)	(.000)	(.000)	(.000)
	[16.1]	[15.6]	[22.2]	[20.8]
Adj. by allotment prob. & weighted real firm size	0.23%	0.08%	1.10%	0.97%
	(.787)	(.867)	(.416)	(.482)
	[4.9]	[4.3]	[7.4]	[7.0]

Table 4.3   **The Expected Percentage Loss From Underwriting (Excluding the Underwriting Concession)**

Shares sold at price on end of	first day	first month
Unweighted by issue size	1.10	1.03
	(.4523)	(.2788)
	[3.17]	[3.09]
Weighted by issue size	0.75	0.67
	(.0043)	(.0000)

Note to tables 4.2 and 4.3: The figure in round parentheses represents the smallest significance level at which the null hypothesis of zero average initial returns would be rejected: that is, the hypothesis is rejected if the chosen significance level is greater than the figure in parenthesis and accepted if the significance level is less than this number. Figure in square parentheses is standard deviation of initial return and weighted initial return. Firm size is adjusted for inflation.

Chapter 5

Distribution and the Efficiency of
New Issue Markets in the US and the UK

Introduction

This chapter tests the hypothesis that investment banks employ a system of distribution which provides a partial control for the adverse selection bias and thus improves the efficiency of new issue markets: investment banks ration new issues in a preferential manner to regular clients to induce them to behave as uninformed investors.

The test of the importance of distribution in determining efficiency exploits institutional and regulatory differences between new issue markets. The following features of the different new issue markets considered in this study are used in formulating the test:

1. The Offer for Sale new issue market: The London Stock Exchange requires that over subscribed issues made by an Offer for Sale be allotted between all investors in proportion to excess demand—all investors must have equal opportunity to obtain shares. That is, the Stock Exchange prohibits preferential rationing to particular groups of investors.

2. The Placement new issue market in the UK: The Placement market is regulated in a similar manner to the Offer for Sale with the exception that the investment bank is free to ration shares in a preferential manner to its regular clients—thus the name Placement. Since the investment bank is free to adopt a system of preferential allotments it is anticipated that this new

issue market is more efficient than the Offer for Sale market. The alternative hypothesis is that the investment bank uses the preferential allotments as a means of extorting monopsony profits from the new issue markets. In this case the Placement market would be more inefficient than the Offer for Sale market.

3.   The IPO new issue market in the US: Investment banks in the IPO new issue market are free to adopt a system of preferential allotments, therefore, it is expected that this market is more efficient than the Offer for Sale. Furthermore, since the syndicate distribution system is more developed in the IPO market it is expected that this market is more efficient than the Placement market in the UK.

This chapter tests the above hypotheses by estimating the uncertainty-under pricing trade-off for each market. It is not possible to test the relative efficiency of new issue markets by comparing the average amount of under pricing since again institutional and regulatory features result in the average uncertainty for issues differing significantly between these markets (see chapter 3 section III). The methodology used is discussed in detail in section I and the estimates are presented in chapter II.

Appendix 3 examines whether the existence of hot issue markets challenges the conclusions concerning the efficiency of new issue markets. Hot issue markets, which have been studied by SEC (1963), Ibbotson and Jaffe (1975) and Ritter (1984), are periods of higher than average initial returns. The appendix provides further tests of Ritter's hypothesis that hot issue markets are equilibrium responses to periods when the average uncertainty surrounding the valuation of new issues increases. The methodology developed in section I enables a more thorough test of the hypothesis than that conducted by Ritter. The results are generally more supportive of the hypothesis than suggested by Ritter.

I.   Estimating the Uncertainty-Under Pricing Trade-Off

This section outlines a methodology for assessing the relative efficiency of different new issue markets by comparing the relationship between the uncertainty of the investment bank in valuing the issue and the average amount of under pricing. One new issue market is defined as being more efficient than another if, adjusting for uncertainty there is less under pricing in that market. The methodology is derived from a similar approach used by Dimson (1979).

To determine this relationship it is necessary to obtain estimates of the degree of uncertainty and the expected amount of under pricing. The estimation procedure must overcome the difficulty that there is only one observation on initial performance for each issue. Consequently, it is necessary to implement a grouping approach for estimating uncertainty and expected under pricing. The approach involves the following steps:

1.   Rank issues by proxies for uncertainty: the proxies used are chosen from information which is publicly available prior to the initial offering and will include information on firm and issue characteristics. Several methods of ranking issues by uncertainty are discussed below.

2.   Obtain group estimates: the observations on the initial return, which have been ranked on the basis of proxies for uncertainty, are divided into n groups of roughly equal size. Group estimates of the expected initial return and ex ante uncertainty are then obtained using the following estimates: Expected initial return is;

$$E[IR]_g = \sum_{j=(g-1)n+1}^{gn} IR_j/n \qquad (5.1)$$

uncertainty is measured as;

$$Var[IR]_g = \frac{\sum_{j=(g-1)n+1}^{gn} (IR_j - E[IR]_g)^2}{n-1} \qquad (5.2)$$

That is, the measure of uncertainty surrounding a group of issues is estimated by examining the dispersion of realised initial returns around the expected market discount.

Ranking Issues by Uncertainty

There are several possible ways of ranking new issues by uncertainty. Ritter (1984) ranked issues by a single proxy. The measures chosen were sales, proxies for size and degree of establishment, and the standard deviation of share price in the first twenty days of trading excluding the offer price. Initial returns are correlated with both of these variables (see Ritter tables 1 to 4). Neither of these proxies are available in the database of UK new issues used in this study.

Dimson (1979) ranked issues by several proxies for uncertainty using a regression model—the methodology used in this study. New issues are then ranked the by fitted initial return predicted by the model. The results of the regression model and the interpretation of the proxies used are presented in table 5.1. The R-squared for the regressions are small, even by normal standards for cross- sectional analysis. However, there is *a priori* reason for expecting such results: If the initial performance could be predicted accurately from publicly available information the hypothesis that under pricing arises from the combined effects of uncertainty and an adverse selection bias would be easily contradicted. Beatty and Ritter (1986) estimate a regression model for initial returns for a sample of new issues conducted in the US and find a similar level of significance in their results. Similar results are obtained by Dimson (1979) for a sample of UK offers for sale.

The regression results presented in table 5.1 are significantly improved when the sample of issues is disaggregated into the sub-samples "investment trusts" and "other issues". For example, the R-squared for these regression models are 24.9% and 22.2% respectively, while the R-squared for the regression with all issues is 13.2%. This indicates that the relationships between these variables and initial return is different for investment trusts and other issues so that the overall fit is reduced when the samples are combined. For this reason it is proposed to use the separate regressions for the ranking of issues by "fitted" initial return—this will be termed the "pooled regression" method of ordering issues by uncertainty.

Estimating the Uncertainty-Under Pricing Trade-off

The linear regression model between group estimates of initial return and uncertainty is estimated to determine the uncertainty-under pricing trade-off:

$$\hat{E}_g[AIR_1] = *.*** + *.*** \, \hat{SD}_g[AIR_1] \tag{5.3}$$

where $E_g[AIR_1]$ is average initial returns for group g and where $SD_g[AIR_1]$ is the standard deviation of the initial returns—the measure of uncertainty for the group. The magnitude of the slope parameter of this regression model forms the estimate of the trade-off between initial returns and uncertainty. The smaller the value of this parameter the more efficient the new issue market.

The *a priori* value for the intercept parameter for model (5.3) is zero—with no uncertainty there is no rational for under pricing. Obtaining an estimated value of this parameter close to zero indicates that the linear model is a suitable one for characterising the relationship —for example if there were a strong non-linear relationship between these variables the estimated intercept would be biased away from zero. In all cases the estimated value of the intercept is close to zero or insignificant, indicating the appropriateness of the linear model.

The above model is estimated for several different group sizes— both for offers for sale and Placements—to provide an indication of the stability of the relationship and the extent of sampling error. While there is some variability in the estimates, in no case is the ranking of relative efficiency affected by the number of groups chosen—compare tables 5.2 and 5.3.

II.   The Relative Efficiency of New Issue Markets

This section present estimates of the uncertainty- under pricing trade-off for the Offer for Sale and Placement new issue markets in the UK and for the IPO new issue market in the US. On the basis of these estimates it is possible to rank the relative efficiency of these markets and test the proposition that the method of distribution is an important determinant of new issue market efficiency. The maintained suggests the following relative efficiency rankings: (1) Offer for sale (UK); (2) Placement (UK); and (3) Initial Public Offering (US).

The Uncertainty-Under Pricing Trade-off for Offers for Sale

Table 5.2 presents estimates of the uncertainty-under pricing trade-off, regression model (5.3), for numbers of groups between 3 and 9. The average of the results obtained is:

$$\hat{E}_g[AIR_1] = -0.109 + 1.350 \, \hat{SD}_g[AIR_1] \qquad (5.4)$$
$$\quad (-2.431) \qquad (4.326)$$

$$\bar{R}^2 = 80.7\%$$

The relationship implies that a 1.0% increase in the standard deviation of expected initial returns—the estimate of the uncertainty of the investment bank concerning the price that will be established in the after market—is matched by an increase of 1.350% in expected initial returns.

The estimate of the uncertainty-under pricing trade-off for the Offer for Sale provides a useful benchmark for testing the relative efficiency of new issue markets because the method of distribution in this market is known and is equivalent to that assumed in the adverse selection model.

The Uncertainty-Under Pricing Trade-off for Placements

The second most frequently used method of making a new issue on the London Stock Exchange is the Placement. The principal difference between the Placement and the Offer for Sale is that the investment bank is free to determine the method of allotment for the issue. Consequently, it is expected that the Placement market is more efficient than the Offer for Sale market.

Stock Exchange regulations limit this method to companies below a certain size. Consequently, the average uncertainty of firms making Placements is larger than for firms making offers for sale. The average under pricing for the 65 issues made by Placement between 1971 and 1980 is 15.45% with standard deviation of 22.62%.

The uncertainty-under pricing trade-off is again estimated for numbers of groups ranging from 3 to 9. The results are presented in table 5.3. The average for these regressions is:

$$\hat{E}_g [AIR_1] = -0.027 + 0.989 \ \hat{SD}_g [AIR_1] \qquad (5.5)$$
$$\qquad (-0.260) \qquad (3.126)$$

$$\bar{R}^2 = 68.3\%$$

That is, a 1% increase in the uncertainty is matched by a 0.989% increase in under pricing. This is significantly less than the 1.350% estimate obtained for offers for sale. This conclusion is in accordance with the hypothesis that the Placement new issue market is more efficient then the Offer for Sale new issue market.

The Uncertainty-Under Pricing Trade-off for the IPO

Ritter's (1984) study of IPOs in the US examines the relationship between initial performance and proxies for ex ante uncertainty. Ritter provides group estimates of average initial performance and standard deviation of initial returns which can be used to estimate the uncertainty- under pricing trade-off in the manner described above. While the method and proxies used to rank issues by uncertainty are different from those used for the Offer for Sale the broad thrust of the methodology is equivalent. The uncertainty-under pricing trade-off is estimated from the categorisation of issues by the standard deviation of initial returns— the group estimates are presented in table 5.4. The regression relationship between these parameter estimates is

$$\hat{E}_g [AIR_1] = -3.604 + 0.592 \ \hat{SD}_g[AIR_1] \qquad (5.6)$$
$$\quad (-1.497) \qquad (14.592)$$

$$\bar{R}^2 = 97.7\% \quad \text{no of groups (g) = 6}$$

The relationship implies that a 1% increase in uncertainty is matched by an increase of only 0.592% in expected initial returns—compared with 1.350% for the Offer for Sale and 0.989% for the Placement in the UK. The regression model also predicts that with zero uncertainty the expected initial return would be -3.604%, however, this parameter estimate is insignificantly different from zero at standard confidence levels.

Thus, again, the evidence is consistent with the maintained hypothesis concerning the importance of the distribution method in new issue markets.

Summary and Conclusion

This chapter provides strong evidence that the method of distribution of new issues has an important bearing on the efficiency of new issue markets. The evidence supports the hypothesis that there is an efficiency gain from investment banks rationing in a preferential manner to regular clients—the rationing scheme provides an incentive for investors to behave as though they were uninformed. The preferential rationing scheme reduces the amount of under pricing required to overcome the adverse selection bias and therefore increases the expected revenue to the issuer. Competition between investment banks for initiation business assures that this system of distribution is adopted.

The specification of the test of the importance of distribution method exploits important regulatory and institutional differences between new issue markets. For the Offer for Sale investment banks are prohibited from rationing in a preferential manner to regular investors. This restriction does not apply in the US. Furthermore, the distribution techniques used in the Placement in the UK are relatively undeveloped compared to the syndication distribution system used in the US for the IPO.

Table 5.1   **Regression Model of the Initial Performance of the Offer for Sale: 1971-1980**

Independent Variable IR_1	All Issues	Investment Trusts only	Other Issues
Constant	0.218 (2.32)	0.574 (4.24)	0.231 (1.74)
Investment Trust Dummy	-0.032 (-1.30)	N/A	N/A
Return on Market Index	1.007 (3.24)	0.987 (1.76)	1.152 (3.24)
Hot Issue Period	0.077 (3.91)	0.033 (1.12)	0.117 (4.86)
Market Capitalisation(log)	0.041 (1.43)	0.025 (0.64)	0.034 (0.89)
Issue Size(log)	-0.065 (-2.15)	-0.025 (-0.98)	-0.049 (-1.20)
Dividend Yield	N/A	N/A	-0.021 (-2.73)
Price Earnings Ratio	N/A	N/A	0.001 (0.74)
$\bar{R}^2$	13.2%	24.9%	22.2%
Durbin Watson Statistic	1.78	1.68	1.73
No of observations	235	58	173

Notes to table 5.1:

The following notes illustrate the rationale for the inclusion of the variables in the above regression:

1. Investment trust dummy: 1 if issue is an investment trust—a closed end mutual fund—or 0 otherwise. The average uncertainty is less for investment trusts since these are most often portfolios of traded securities or property investments;

2. Return on market index: change in the Financial Times 100 index form the date of the publication of the prospectus to the close of the first day of trading. Parameter estimate is unity for investment trusts reflecting the portfolio nature of these investments. The parameter estimate is higher for other issues reflecting the higher than average systematic risk of new issues;

3. Hot issue period: 1 if the last three issues experienced positive initial returns, 0 for first three issues and 0 otherwise. The empirical rationale for this variable is suggested by the analysis of Ibbotson and Jaffe (1975), Dimson (1979) and Ritter (1984);

4. Market capitalisation: market value of shareholders equity—issues and held by initial owners—valued at the offer price. This is a proxy for firms size so that we would expect a negative parameter estimate;

5. Issue size: this variable could be acting as a proxy for firm size;

6. Dividend yield: issue price per share divided by dividend per share at issue. In general more established companies pay higher dividends. Therefore, it is expected that dividend yield is negatively related to uncertainty; and

7. Price earnings ratio: issue price divided by earnings per share at issue. The larger the PE ratio the greater are the growth prospects which are being discounted in the share price therefore the greater the uncertainty.

Table 5.2 The Uncertainty-Under Pricing Trade-off for Offers for Sale in the UK

Number of groups	Intercept (t-stat)	Slope (t-stat)	$\bar{R}^2$
3	-0.145% (-2.430)	1.618% (3.840)	93.7%
4	-0.105% (-2.470)	1.289% (4.460)	90.9%
5	-0.123% (-3.820)	1.444% (6.450)	93.3%
6	-0.128% (-2.990)	1.530% (5.010)	86.2%
7	-0.099% (-2.100)	1.258% (3.910)	75.3%
8	-0.070% (-1.450)	1.071% (3.190)	62.9%
9	-0.090% (-1.760)	1.242% (3.420)	62.5%
Average	-0.109% (-2.431)	1.350% (4.326)	80.7%

Note: derived using the grouping methodology derived in section I.

Table 5.3   **The   Uncertainty-Under   Pricing   Trade-off   for Placements in the UK**

Number of groups	Intercept (t-stat)	Slope (t-stat)	$\bar{R}^2$
3	-0.088% (-2.030)	1.410% (5.730)	97.0%
4	-0.130% (-0.170)	0.970% (2.290)	73.4%
5	-0.003% (-0.040)	0.910% (2.290)	69.6%
6	0.028% (0.470)	0.770% (2.290)	56.7%
7	0.008% (0.130)	0.900% (2.760)	60.3%
8	0.013% (0.130)	0.940% (2.570)	52.4%
9	-0.014% (-0.310)	1.020% (3.950)	69.0%
Average	-0.027% (0.260)	0.989% (3.126)	68.3%

Note: derived using the grouping methodology derived in section I.

Table 5.4   Ritter's Estimates of the Relationship between Initial Performance and a Proxy for Uncertainty

Category [% hot/tot hot]	1977-82	Hot-issue	Cold Issue
0.000<sd<.024 [8.4]	6.4% (20.7)	12.4% (21.5)	5.2% (20.3)
0.024<sd<.033 [11.3]	9.7% (23.3)	9.8% (20.7)	9.7% (24.1)
0.033<sd<.043 [18.3]	14.6% (26.5)	23.0% (36.6)	10.0% (17.4)
0.043<sd<.057 [21.5]	28.1% (58.6)	46.7% (80.0)	14.4% (29.2)
0.057<sd<.076 [18.6]	39.1% (65.2)	67.4% (83.5)	21.3% (42.0)
0.076<sd [21.9]	59.5% (108.3)	92.6% (141.4)	33.7% (62.4)
All issues [100.0]	26.3% (62.0)	49.2% (90.4)	14.7% (35.5)

Note: Standard Deviation of initial returns in parentheses. The standard deviations have been computed using the first 20 daily returns in the after market—excluding initial returns. Source table 3 of Ritter (1984).

Chapter 6

Summary and Conclusions

The central theme of this thesis has been the examination of the efficiency of new issue markets. The thesis examines efficiency from two perspectives:

1.   Efficiency conditions implied by the adverse selection model: strong evidence is provided that uninformed investors and investment banks do not realise excess returns from new issue markets. The test is conducted using the Offer for Sale new issue market because of the regulations governing distribution and the availability of information on the demand for each issue.

2.   Distribution and the efficiency of new issue markets: this thesis develops and tests the first economic explanation of the role of distribution in determining the efficiency of new issue markets. It presents strong evidence that investment banks use the ability to ration shares in a preferential manner to reduce the expected costs of under pricing to the issuing company.

The research contained in this thesis suggests further topics for economic research into the operation of the investment banking industry:

1.   Syndicate distribution techniques in the US: no where has there been a detailed economic analysis of the operation of the syndicate distribution systems in the US. The theory of the role of distribution developed in this thesis should provide a useful starting point for this analysis.

2.   Efficiency and investment bank reputation: the empirical methodology developed in chapter 5 could be applied to examine the question of whether the more "reputable" investment banks are more efficient at distributing new issues —are their distribution systems better at controlling the adverse selection bias in the new issue market? A related issue, is whether such a difference gave rise to the hot issue market of 1980. Or, is it the case, as Ritter (1984) suggests, that this is an instance of investment banks exploiting monopsony power.

3.   The relative efficiency of tender offers: the methodology for assessing the relative efficiency of new issue markets should be applied to tender offers. With tender offers the investment bank cannot operate a system of preferential allotments. Under pricing is the only way to compensate the uninformed for the adverse selection bias created by the more informed participants in the tender offer. Perhaps as uncertainty increases the relative efficiency gain from employing the system of preferential allotments out-weighs the gain from having investors reveal information by competitive bidding. Perhaps this theory can account for the empirical observation that large established firms tend to be the most frequent users of tenders.

The Nature of the Information Asymmetry in New Issue Markets

Introduction

The crucial assumption of the adverse selection model is that regarding the existence of the two classes of investors. The issuer, uninformed investors and the investment bank are assumed to be uncertain about the value of the issue and informed investors have perfect information. While the distinction between informed and uninformed investors is clearly an extreme assumption it is a simple way to represent an information structure where one group of investors has privileged access to information—this privileged group need not have perfect information.

The most contentious aspect of this specification of the information asymmetry is not that the investment bank is uncertain about firm value but rather that some investors have superior information relative to the investment bank. This assumption lacks intuitive appeal because the investment bank/issuer would appear to have superior access to information given its involvement in the initiation of the issue. Initiation entails a detailed examination of the company, its accounts, its markets, its principal contracts, its management, the rating of similar firms in the market etc. The investigation which the investment bank conducts uncovers much information about the firm and its management which is not published in the prospectus for the issue.

Rock offers several reasons for treating the issuer as uninformed—that is having less information than informed investors. "First, the firm and investment bank give up their proprietary information to the market...... Second, even though the firm and its agents know more than any single individual, they know less than all the individuals in the market combined...... Some individuals may have inside information about a competitor that could have a significant impact upon the firm's product. Others may know better than the banker the appropriate rate to discount the firm's cash flow in the capital market." (p. 190)

It will be demonstrated below that it is not necessary for informed investors to have superior access to information, relative to the investment bank, for an adverse selection bias to exist against uninformed investors. It will be shown that it is sufficient for one group of investors to have superior information relative to another group even if both groups do not have as much information as the investment bank.

Information in this context refers to the distribution of the estimate used to assess firm value. The more information which an agent has the smaller the variance of this distribution.

I.   The Adverse Selection Model When the Informed do not have Perfect Information

The essence of the adverse selection bias in new issue markets is that 1. investors make independent assessments of the value of an issue before deciding whether or not to subscribe and 2. some investors are better at such assessments than others. It is not necessary that some investors have superior information relative to the initiating investment bank.

The specification of the adverse selection model where the informed produce an independent estimate of v, denoted VI recognises the possibility of stochastic informed demand. The empirical estimates of informed demand in chapter 4 illustrate that it is in fact highly stochastic (see table 4.1). The usefulness of considering this specification of informed demand is also suggested by the finding, in chapter 2, that under pricing is not rational where perfectly informed demand is twice issue size (see chapter 2 section II).

We do not propose to develop an equilibrium model of under pricing with stochastic informed demand because of the complexities of the model required. Instead, the aim of this section is to demonstrate in a simple model that with stochastic informed demand it is not necessary for the informed to have more information relative to the investment bank for an adverse selection bias to exist against the uninformed. This proposition will be demonstrated by adapting the adverse selection model as follows:

1.   the investment bank, B, and the informed investors, I, each produce an estimate of v from the distribution $f_j(v)$ where $j = B$ and I. All of the informed produce the same estimate vI which is independent of v_B. The estimates are drawn from uniform distributions: that is, $V_B \sim U(-b/2, b/2)$ with variance $Var[V_B] = b^2/12$ (similarly for v_I).

2.   informed investors apply for the issue with their whole wealth if $v_I > p$. Uninformed investors apply for all issues with the fraction T of their wealth: that is we do not attempt to demonstrate an equilibrium model of the level of informed and uninformed demand.

Thus in this formulation of the adverse selection model informed investors do not have perfect information of v—they too must form an estimate of share value. Both the informed and the investment bank are interpreted as forming point estimates of the value of the share. These estimates are assumed to be independent.

For this set of assumptions the probabilities of allotment are as follows: the probability of allotment when only uninformed investors apply is

$$p_N = \min\{pZ/NT, 1\} \qquad\qquad (A.1.1)$$

and when all investors apply it is

$$p_{IN} = \min\{pZ/(NT+I), 1\} \qquad\qquad (A.1.2)$$

Since it is the aim of this section to demonstrate conditions for which an adverse selection bias exists, it is sufficient to demonstrate the existence of negative expected gains to uninformed investors when the investment bank does not under price issues—therefore, it is assumed that $d = 0$.

Given the above assumptions the following theorems and corollaries are demonstrated in the mathematical appendix.

Theorem A.1.1

For uninformed investors the expected gain from new issue subscription is

$$E_U[\text{gain}] = (p_{IU} - p_U) \cdot \frac{1}{i} \cdot \frac{b^2}{12} \; < \; 0 \qquad\qquad (A.1.3)$$

since $p_U > p_{IU}$.

Corollary

1. As the variance of the informed investor's estimate rises, the magnitude of the uninformed investor's expected loss falls. (The variance of the informed investor's estimate is given by $i^2/12$).
2. As the variance of the investment bank's estimate ($b^2/12$) falls, the magnitude of the uninformed investor's expected loss falls.

Theorem A.1.2

For informed investors

$$E_I[\text{gain}] = p_{IU} \frac{1}{i} \frac{b^2}{12} \; > \; 0 \qquad\qquad (A.1.4)$$

That is, the informed investor realises a gain from the sorting activity. This gain is positive irrespective of the relative magnitude of $\text{Var}[V_B]$ and $\text{Var}[V_I]$.

Theorem A.1.3

$$E[\text{total gain}] = ((NT+I)p_{IU}\text{-}NTp_U) \frac{1}{i} \frac{b^2}{12} \qquad\qquad (A.1.5)$$

Corollary

1.   If all issues are over subscribed then E[total gain] = 0, by substituting (A.1.1) and (A.1.2) into (A.1.5). That is, the expected gain to the informed is exactly equal to the expected loss for the uninformed when all issues are over subscribed.
2.   If all issues for which only uninformed investors apply are under subscribed then E[total gain] > 0.

The intuition behind these results is as follows:

1.   the expected total gain to all investors and the investment bank sums to zero since the investment bank's estimate was assumed to be unbiased, shares are not offered at an expected discount and the underwriting concession is assumed to be zero. In the situation where all issues are over subscribed the investment bank incurs no losses as a result of underwriting. Therefore the expected gains to the informed arise solely as a result of imposing equivalent expected losses on the uninformed; and
2.   issues which are under subscribed impose an expected loss on the investment bank. This reduces the size of the uninformed loss. Thus the combined expected total gain of informed and uninformed investors which is positive equals the size of the expected loss imposed on the investment bank from its underwriting activity.

These results can be easily generalised to the case where the uninformed also produce an independent estimate of v but have a larger variance attaching to their estimate. In this case the expected return for the uninformed may be positive or negative—the expected return is negative when the adverse selection losses caused by the better informed investors are greater than the sorting gains for the uninformed.

The possibility that the uninformed also make an independent assessment of firm value provides a further possible solution to the apparent contradiction raised in chapter 2—specifically that under pricing is irrational when perfectly informed demand is more than twice issue size. The solution is that the uninformed may also realise gains from sorting so that the amount of under pricing required to compensate them for the bias and ensure a zero expected return is reduced relative to the case where they apply for all issues.

A conclusion from this hypothesis is that issues with larger negative initial returns should be more under subscribed. Chapter 4 presents evidence that this is not the case (see (4.2)). We conclude therefore that the rationality of the under pricing equilibrium, given the observed level of average informed demand, rests in the observation that the adverse selection model overstates the information advantage of the informed.

This simple model demonstrates the existence of an adverse selection bias against uninformed investors even for the case where informed investors are not as well informed as the investment bank. The adverse selection bias arises from the fact that 1. some or all investors make independent assessments of share value and 2. some investors are better at making such assessments than others. When the investment bank over estimates the value of the firm by a large amount it is more likely that the better informed investors will place a lower value on the firm and thus refrain from applying for the issue. The lesser informed investors are more likely to apply for the issue than the better informed. This situation is sufficient to create an adverse selection bias against the lesser informed investor. This bias exists whether or not the better informed investors can produce an estimate with a smaller variance attaching to it than the investment bank.

An implication of this specification of the information asymmetry is a negatively sloped demand function for new issues. Ceteris paribus the lower the offer price set by the investment bank the higher the probability that the estimate produced by a randomly chosen investor will exceed that value and consequently the higher the probability that the investor will apply for the issue. Thus the lower the offer price the higher the expected number of investors that will apply for the issue. The negatively sloped demand reflects the fact that investors make independent assessments of firm value.

The adverse selection bias arises from the fact that investors have differing abilities in making such assessments. That investors have differing abilities in assessing new issues is a point which can be taken for granted—the professional (institutional) investor is surely a shrewder judge of new issue value than the private investor. Thus, the existence of a negatively sloped demand for new issues substantiates the existence of an adverse selection bias against lesser informed investors. Chapter 4 presents evidence of such a negatively sloped demand.

The Identity of Informed Demand

Before leaving the discussion of the information structure of new issue markets it is informative to speculate as to the identity of informed investors. Informed investors are those whose application is correlated with initial performance. We consider three hypotheses regarding the identity of the informed:

1.   The institutional or professional investors who participate in new issue markets generally have better experience of the market and access to security analysis. These investors may be long term investors but can form a good view on when to buy a particular stock. In Ireland and the UK the level of institutional demand can vary significantly from issue to issue. This is especially the case for actively managed or performance equity funds.

2.   "Stags"—investors who take a very short term view and speculate on the price of the issue in early trading. The following excerpts from a Financial Times article illustrate the behaviour of the stag: "You have to sell within the first half-hour. The golden rule is that if you are a stag stick to staging.... arrange a line of bank credit..... [one stag is quoted as saying to his bank manager] 'I want to stag. I'll give you a second mortgage on my house'....... The big people use millions" (Financial Times August 16 1986 p 7). Stags are individual investors who feel close enough to new issue markets to risk large sums. They may themselves be employed as professional investors but also come from other professions—a barrister is quoted in the F.T. article as saying that he lost money only once in two years of staging.

3.   Alternatively, it could be argued that insiders to the issue are the better informed investors —managers and owners may be able to assess when the investment bank has undervalued the issue. The adverse selection bias could conceivably arise from the fact that when they assess that the issue is undervalued they purchase extra shares and advise outsiders of their findings. This interpretation of the adverse selection model lacks much intuitive appeal. Firstly, the size of management's preferential allotment is limited to a small fraction of the issue. Secondly, empirical evidence in chapter 4 shows that there is enormous variation in the demand for new issues—insiders are unlikely to be able to command sufficient wealth to cause such variation. Also it is unlikely that management could communicate their belief effectively to such large amounts of outside wealth because of their moral hazard incentive to provide information to support the issue.

We do not present a test to distinguish the most important source of informed demand. We do however test the relationship that informed demand is positively related to the uncertainty, a determinant of the gains to becoming informed. It is argued in chapter 2 that this relationship supports Rock's formulation of the model where the informed incur a cost to become informed and in equilibrium the expected gain to the marginal uninformed investor is zero.

Appendix 2

Mathematical Appendix

I.   Mathematical Appendix to Chapter 2

Theorem 2.1

$$E[W] = 1 + (T/p)E\{V\text{-}P\,|\,A\}P\{A\}, \text{ where}$$

$$E\{V\text{-}p\,|\,A\}P\{A\} = E\{V\text{-}p\,|\,V>p\}bP\{V>p\}$$
$$+ E\{V\text{-}p\,|\,V<p\}b'P\{V<p\}$$

Proof

$$E[W] = E\{W\,|\,A\}bP\{V>p\} + E\{W\,|\,A\}b'P\{V<p\}$$
$$+E\{W\,|\,B\}(1\text{-}b)P\{V>p\} + E\{W\,|\,B\}(1\text{-}b)'P\{V<p\}$$

On allotment $W = 1+T(V\text{-}p)/p$ and otherwise $W = 1$. The remainder of the proof follows by noting that

$$E\{1+T(V\text{-}p)/p\,|\,V>p\}bP\{V>p\}$$
$$= bP\{V>p\} + (T/p)E\{V\text{-}p\,|\,V>p\}bP\{V>p\}, \text{ and}$$

$$1 = bP\{V>p\} + (1\text{-}b)P\{V>p\} + b'P\{V<p\}$$
$$+ (1\text{-}b')P\{V<p\}$$

Theorem 2.2

$b_0(p)$ satisfies the following properties:

1. $\qquad b_o(p) \; < \; 1 \quad \text{as } p < E[V]$
$\qquad\qquad\quad = \; 1 \quad \text{as } p = E[V]$
$\qquad\qquad\quad > \; 1 \quad \text{as } p > E[V]$

2. $\quad \lim\limits_{p \to 0} b_o(p) \; = \; 0$

3. $\qquad b'(p) \; > \; 0$

Proof

1. The proof of the proposition follows from the fact that

$$E\{V-E[V] \mid V<E[V]\}P\{V<E[V]\} \;=\; \{E[V]-V \mid V>E[V]\}P\{V>E[V]\}$$

$$= \int_0^{E[V]} (v-E[V])f(v)d(v)$$

$$= (E[V] - \int_{E[V]}^{\infty} vf(v)d(v)) - E[V]F(E[V])$$

$$= E[V](1 - F(E[V])) - \int_{E[V]}^{\infty} vf(v)dv$$

$$= E[V] \int_{E[V]}^{\infty} f(v)dv - \int_{E[V]}^{\infty} vf(v)dv$$

$$= \int_{E[V]}^{\infty} (E[V] - v)f(v)dv$$

$$= E\{E[V]-V \mid V>E[V]\}P\{V>E[V]\}$$

2. As p approaches 0, the numerator of $b_o(p)$ tends to

$$\int_{o}^{0} (0-v)f(v)dv = 0$$

and the denominator tends to

$$\int_{o}^{0} (v-0)f(v)dv = E[V]$$

hence, $b_o(p)$ approaches $0/E[V] = 0$ as p approaches zero.

3. $$b_o(p) = \frac{E\{p-V\,|\,V<p\}P\{V<p\}}{E\{V-p\,|\,V>p\}P\{V>p\}}$$

$E\{V-p|V>p\}P\{V>p\}$

$$= \int_{p}^{\infty} (v-p)f(v)dv$$

$$= \int_{\infty}^{p} (p-v)f(v)dv$$

$$\frac{d\,E\{V-p\,|\,V>p\}P\{V>p\}}{dp} = -pf(p) + pf(p) - \int_{p}^{\infty} f(v)dv = -P\{V>p\}$$

Similarly,

$$\frac{d\,E\{V-p\,|\,V<p\}P\{V<p\}}{dp} = P\{V<p\}$$

The expression for $b'_o(p)$ follows by using the rule for the derivative of a quotient and the above rules

$$b'_o(p)=\frac{E\{V-p\,|\,V>p\}P\{V>p\}P\{V<p\}-E\{p-V\,|\,p>V\}P\{p>V\}(-P\{V>p\})}{E\{V-p\,|\,V>p\}P\{V>p\}E\{V-p\,|\,V>p\}P\{V>p\}}>0$$

Theorem 2.3

1. $\quad \lim_{p \to 0} g(p) = 0$, where $g(p) = b_o(p)/p$

2. $\quad g'(p) > 0$

Proof

1. Both the numerator and the denominator of $b_o(p)$ tend to zero as p approaches zero so that we must use l'Hopital's rule which states that

$$\lim_{p \to 0} g(p) = \frac{\lim p \to 0 \, u'(p)}{\lim p \to 0 \, v'(p)}, \text{ where}$$

$$\lim p \to 0 \, u(p) = \lim p \to 0 \, v(p) = 0.$$

Substitution of 0 for p in the definition of $b'_o(p)$ in theorem 2.2 yields the conclusion

$$\lim_{p \to 0} b'_o(p) = \frac{E[V].1.0 - 0.0.-1}{(E[V].1)^2} = 0$$

The derivative of the denominator of $g(p)$ is 1, hence $g(p)$ tends to zero as p approaches zero.

2. Since the logarithmic function is a monotonic transformation it is sufficient to demonstrate that $G'(p) > 0$ where $G(p) = \ln(g(p))$

$$G'(p) = \frac{d \ln(b_o(p))}{dp} - \frac{1}{p}$$

Using the rule for the derivative of the function ln(.) and the relationships used in the proof of theorem 2.2.3. it follows that

$$\frac{d \ln(b_o(p))}{dp} = \frac{1}{E\{p-V|p>V\}} + \frac{1}{E\{p-V|p<V\}}$$

Both of the expectations in this equation are positive for all p. Since the expectation $E\{p - V|p>V\}$ cannot exceed p it follows that this derivative is greater than $1/p$.

Theorem 2.4

$$r(p) = Z.E[V] - I \int_0^p (1-v/p)f(v)dv, \text{ in the range } [p_l, p_o].$$

Proof

$$r(p) = E\{\text{revenue} \mid \text{under pricing}\}P\{\text{under pricing}\}$$
$$+ E\{\text{revenue} \mid \text{overpricing}\}P\{\text{overpricing}\}$$

$$= pZ(1-F(p))$$
$$+E\{NT^*(p)+V[Z-NT^*(p)/p)] \mid p>V\}P\{p>V\}$$

$$= Z(E[V]- \int_p^\infty (v-p)f(v)dv)+ NT^*(p) \int_0^p (1-v/p)f(v)dv$$

This is the formulation of $r(p)$ used to derive (2.11).

$$= Z(E[V]- \int_p^\infty (v-p)f(v)dv)+ \left(\frac{Z}{g(p)} - I\right)\int_0^p (1-v/p)f(v)dv$$

by substitution from the definition of the uninformed demand function in the range $[p_f, p_o]$—see (2.6).

$$= Z(E[V] - \int_p^\infty (v-p)f(v)dv) + \frac{Z}{b_o(p)}\int_0^p (p-v)f(v)dv - I \int_0^p (1-v/p)f(v)dv$$

$$= Z(E[V] - \int_p^\infty (v-p)f(v)dv) + Z\left(\frac{\int_p^\infty (v-p)f(v)dv}{\int_0^p (p-v)f(v)dv} \right) \int_0^p (p-v)f(v)dv$$

$$-I\int_0^P (1-v/p)f(v)dv$$

by substitution from derivation of (2.2) in theorem 2.2. Finally, by cancellation:

$$= ZE[V] - I \int_0^P (1-v/p)f(v)dv$$

Theorem 2.5

$$p_C/j(p_C) = E[V] + (1/3)E[V] + (4/9)(E[V]-a)$$

Proof

The proof of this proposition follows from the following definitions:

1. $$p_C = E[V] - \int_{E[V]}^\infty (v-E[V])f(v)dv$$

$$= E[V] - a/4, \text{ from } (2.11).$$

2. $$b_o(p) = \frac{E[V \mid V<p].P[V<p]}{E[V \mid V>p].P[V>p]}$$

from the definition of $b_o(p)$ in (2.2) and theorem 2.2.

$$= \frac{0.5(p-(E[V]-a)).0.5a(p-(E[V]-a))}{0.5(E[V]+a-p).0.5a(E[V]+a-p)}$$

$$= \frac{(p-E[V]+a)^2}{(E[V]+a-p)^2}$$

3. $$j(p) = \frac{b_o(p)}{1-b_o(p)}$$

The remainder of the proof follows by simple substitution.

II.   Mathematical Appendix to Appendix 1

This appendix provides a demonstration of the propositions advanced in appendix 1. A general expression for the expected gain from new issue subscription must take account of the probability that $v_B = V_B$, the probability that an investor applies for the issue and the probability that the investor is allotted shares in the issue. The expression for the expected gain is

$$E[gain] = \int_{-\infty}^{\infty} (v-p)P[V_B=v_B \ \& \ applied \ and \ allotted]dv$$

where $p = v_B-d$. Using the definition for conditional probability it follows that

$$E[gain] = \int_{-\infty}^{\infty} (v-p)P[V_B=v_B]xP[applied \mid V_B=v_B] \ x$$

$$P[allotted \mid applied \ and \ V_B=v_B]dv$$

For expositional simplicity we assume that $v = 0$. This can be rationalised by assuming that v changes hands initially and that the pricing of the issue involves transactions about this level—that is rebates or additional payments for investors. The following definitions are implied by the assumption that $f(v)$ is uniformly distributed on $(v-b/2, v+b/2)$.

$$f(v) = \begin{pmatrix} 1/b & \text{for } -b/2 < v_B < b/2 \\ 0 & \text{otherwise} \end{pmatrix}$$

$$F(v) = \frac{v_B + b/2}{b}, \quad -b/2 < v_B < b/2$$

$$1 - F(v) = \frac{b/2 - v_B}{b}, \quad -b/2 < v_B < b/2$$

and similarly for V_I.

Theorem A.1.1

For uninformed investors

$$E_U[\text{gain}] = (p_{IU} - p_U) \cdot \frac{1}{i} \cdot \frac{b^2}{12} < 0$$

Proof

Note the following identities:

$p[\text{applied} \mid V_B = v_B] = 1$ since uninformed always apply; and

$p[\text{allotted} \mid \text{applied}, V_B = v_B]$

$\qquad\qquad = p[\text{allotted} \mid \text{all apply}, V_B = v_B] p[\text{I apply}]$
$\qquad\qquad + p[\text{allotted} \mid \text{I don't apply}, V_B = v_B] p[\text{I don't apply}]$

$\qquad\qquad = p_{IU} \cdot [1 - F_I(v_B)] + p_U \cdot F(v_B)$

$\qquad\qquad = p_{IU} + (p_U - p_{IU}) \frac{v_B + i/2}{i}$

Substituting these expressions into the general expression for the expected gain above (with $d = 0$ or $p = V_B$ and $v = 0$)

$$E \text{ [gain]} = -v_B \cdot \frac{1}{b} \cdot [p_{IU} + (p_U - p_{IU}) \frac{v_B + i/2}{i}].1.dv_B$$

$$= (p_{IU} - p_U) \cdot \frac{1}{i} \cdot \frac{b^2}{12}$$

This completes the proof.

Theorem A.1.2

For informed investors,

$$E_I \text{[gain]} = p_{IU} \frac{1}{i} \cdot \frac{b^2}{12}$$

Proof:

Note the following definitions:

$$p[\text{applied} \mid V_B = v_B] = p[V_I > v_B] = 1 - F_I(v_B) = \frac{i/2 - v_B}{i} \text{ ; and}$$

$p[\text{allotted} \mid \text{applied}, V_B = v_B] = p_{IU}$ since if one informed investor applies it is assumed that all informed investors apply.

Substituting these definitions into (A.1.1)

$$E_I \text{[gain]} = v_B \cdot \frac{1}{b} \cdot p_{IU} \cdot \frac{i/2 - v_B}{i} dv$$

$$= p_{IU} \frac{1}{i} \cdot \frac{b^2}{12}$$

This completes the proof.

Theorem A.1.3

$$E \text{[total gain]} = \left((NT + I)p_{IU} - NTp_U\right) \frac{1}{i} \cdot \frac{b^2}{12}$$

Proof

$$E[\text{total gain}] = w_I E_I[\text{gain}] + w_U E_U[\text{gain}]$$

where w_j is the weight in total demand $j = I$ and U. The proof follows by substituting (A.1.4) and (A.1.5) into this expression.

Appendix 3

Hot Issue Markets

Introduction

Hot issue markets, which are defined as periods of higher than average initial returns, have been studied by the SEC (1963), Ibbotson and Jaffe (1975) and by Ritter (1984). Ritter has provided the only equilibrium explanation of the hot issue phenomenon which is based on the application of the adverse selection model of the type developed in chapter 2.

Ritter's hypothesis is that hot issue periods are a reflection of:

1.   A stable relationship between uncertainty and under pricing as predicted by the adverse selection model.
2.   A change in the average risk composition of new issues.

Hot issue markets are explained as periods when average uncertainty is greater than usual.

Ritter tests this hypothesis by ranking issues by proxies for uncertainty—he chooses sales and the standard deviation of the after market price. Table 5.4 presents his new issue rankings by the standard deviation of prices in the after market—excluding the offer price. The evidence in table 5.4 provides some support for the hypothesis that hot issue periods are caused an increase in the average uncertainty of firms making IPOs: a higher proportion of the hot issues are in the categories which imply higher than average uncertainty (as illustrated by column one of table 5.4).

However, the finding that average under pricing within each standard deviation category is significantly higher leads Ritter to reject the hypothesis of a stable trade off between uncertainty and under pricing. This appendix evaluates this conclusion using the methodology for estimating the uncertainty-under pricing trade-off developed in section I.

I.   Uncertainty-Under Pricing Trade-Off in Hot Issue Markets

Ritter interprets the increase in the average amount of under pricing within each of the categories as evidence of a non-stationarity in the uncertainty-under pricing trade-off during hot issue markets. However, it is clear from table 5.4 that the standard deviation of initial returns within each category also increases. Since the standard deviation of initial returns is arguably the best proxy for uncertainty it not certain whether these higher average initial returns represent a shift in the uncertainty-under pricing trade-off.

In fact, the estimation of the trade-off using the grouping methodology developed in section I shows that there is no statistically significant difference in the relationship between initial returns and uncertainty between hot and cold issue periods. The estimates of the uncertainty-under pricing trade-off using the data in table 5.4 are presented in table A.3.1. In cold issue markets a 1.0% increase in uncertainty   results in a 0.596% increase in under pricing. The equivalent change in hot issue markets in 0.692%. This is a statistically insignificant difference at the 5.0% confidence level. Average under pricing in the cold issue markets is 14.7% and average under pricing in the hot issue markets is 49.2%. Clearly, this represents very strong evidence in favour of Ritter's hypothesis. The evidence in table A.3.1 illustrates that there is a non-stationarity in the relationship between the proxies for uncertainty and actual uncertainty.

This finding suggests that more analysis be conducted on the sample of IPOs studied by Ibbotson and Ritter using the grouping methodology outlined in section I. Further verifying Ritter's hypothesis would provide another important piece of evidence concerning the efficiency of new issue markets in addition to that provided by this thesis.

Before concluding this discussion we examine Ritter's assertion that the hot issue market of 1980 is due to a non- stationarity in the uncertainty-under pricing trade-off for natural resource new issues.

II.   The Hot Issue Market of 1980: Natural Resource Issues

Table A.3.2 presents estimates of the uncertainty-under pricing trade-off for natural resource and non-natural resource issues for hot issue and cold issue periods. The estimates, which are derived from the groupings contained in Ritter's table 4, suggest the following points:

1.   the uncertainty-under pricing trade-off for cold natural resource issues is similar to all non- natural resource issues: 0.506% against 0.568%; and

2.   there is a distinct natural resource effect between hot and cold issue periods: for the hot issue period the trade off is 1.062% as against 0.506% for the cold issue period or 0.592% for all issues (table A.3.1).

Ritter examines several alternative hypotheses for this non-stationarity in the uncertainty-under pricing trade-off:

1.   institutional lags between the setting of the offer price and commencement of trading in a rising market;

2.   speculative bubble: issues were priced correctly but investors expectations were speculative; and

3.   monopsony power hypothesis: underwriters intentionally under price the issues and earn profits by allocating these issues only to favoured customers.

Ritter concludes that the monopsony power hypothesis explains the hot issue effect for natural resources:

> The monopsony power hypothesis is implicitly a market-segmentation hypothesis. Since only natural resource issues were excessively under priced during the hot issue market of 1980, other firms were not subject to this exploitation.....(page 236). Natural resource issues may have been subject to this monopsony exploitation during the hot issue market of 1980 because of the concentration of these issuers in a regional (Denver) market (page 232).

An alternative explanation to the monopsony power hypothesis is that the investment banks who brought these firms to market did not have as well developed distribution systems as reflected by the average distribution capacity in the market. That is, their rationing schemes did not assure as high a probability of allotment to the uninformed as was the case for the "average investment bank". The investment banks who initiate most of the small issues are small regional banks without access the a developed syndication system. There is ample casual evidence that "reputable" investment banks, who are the frequent participants in the syndicate system of distribution, generally avoid highly speculative issues for example Waterman 1958).

A possible test of the hypothesis would be to estimate the uncertainty-under pricing trade-off for issues conducted by the small regional investment banks. If this approximates the trade-off for the natural resource issues during the 1980 hot issue market the monopsony power hypothesis would be rejected. The effect of reputation on the efficiency of new issue markets is a potentially fruitful area for further research.

A concluding insight on the possible validity of the monopsony power hypothesis is gained by comparing the estimated uncertainty-under pricing trade-off for natural resource hot issues with the trade-off for offers for sale in the UK. Extensive tests of the efficiency of Offer for Sale new issue markets could not reject the hypothesis of efficiency despite the fact that the estimated uncertainty- under pricing trade-off is 1.350% as against 1.062% for hot issue natural resource issues. This 1.062% trade-off is similar to the 0.989% estimated for Placements in the UK.

III.   Conclusions

This appendix has established the finding of Ritter that there was a non-stationarity in the uncertainty-under pricing trade-off for natural resource issues during the 1980 hot issue market. However, it was not of sufficient magnitude to significantly affect the uncertainty-under pricing trade-off for all new issues (see table A.3.1).

It has also suggested an alternative to the monopsony power hypothesis which can be tested by examining how the nature of the uncertainty-under pricing trade-off changes with respect to the type of investment bank initiating the issue.

Table A.3.1   The Uncertainty-Under Pricing Trade-off for IPOs in the US: Hot Issue Market Effects

	Intercept (t-stat)	Slope (t-stat)	$\bar{R}^2$
All issues	-3.604% (-1.497)	0.592% (14.569)	97.7%
Hot issues	-2.243% (-0.408)	0.692% (10.401)	95.5%
Cold issues	-3.704% (-1.635)	0.596% (9.492)	94.7%

Table A.3.2   The Uncertainty-Under Pricing Trade-off for Natural and Non-Natural Resource Issues

	Intercept (t-stat)	Slope (t-stat)	$\bar{R}^2$
Natural Resource Issues:			
all issues	-9.69% (-1.608)	0.757% (10.780)	95.8%
hot issues	-6.517% (-0.480)	1.062% (7.684)	92.1%
cold issues	-2.502% (-1.511)	0.506% (13.633)	97.4%
Non-Natural Resource Issues:			
all issues	-0.718% (-0.219)	0.568% (5.957)	87.3%
hot issues	0.433% (1.598)	0.417% (3.873)	73.7%
cold issues	-3.800% (-1.290)	0.650% (7.172)	91.0%

Note to table A.3.1 and A.3.2: derived using the grouping methodology derived in section I. Group estimates obtained from Ritter 4.

Bibliography

Baron, David P (1982). A Model of the Demand for Investment Banking Advising and Distribution Services for New Issues. *Journal of Finance*, September.

Barzel, Yorman (1977). Some Fallacies in the Interpretation of Information. *Journal of Law and Economics*, October.

Bear, R.M. and Curley, A.J. (1975). Unseasoned Equity Financing. *Journal of Financial and Quantitative Analysis*, pp. 311-25.

Beatty Randolph P. and Ritter, Jay R. (1986) Investment Banking, Reputation, and the Under Pricing of Initial Public Offerings. *Journal of Financial Economics*, pp. 213-32.

Blaser, A.L. (1971). *Dynamic Price Movements: The New Issues After market*. Ph. D Thesis, University of Oregon.

Blaum, J.D. (1971). *Analysis of the Price Behaviour of Initial Common Stock Offerings*. Ph. D Thesis, Michigan State University.

Carosso, Vincent P. (1970). *Investment Banking in America: A History. Cambridge*, Mass., Harvard University Press.

Clurman (1970). Controlling a Hot Issue Market. *Cornell Law Review*, pp. 74-78.

Cooke, Gibert W. et al (1962). *Financial Institutions: Their Role in the American Economy*. New York, N.Y., Simmons-Boardman Publishing Corporation.

Darby, Michael R. and Lott John R. (1983). Qualitative Information, Reputation and Monopolistic Competition. University of California, Los Angeles, Discussion Paper no. 265.

Davey, Patrick J. (9176). *Investment Banking Arrangements*. New York, N.Y., The Conference Board Inc.

Dimson, Elroy (1978). *The Efficiency of of the British New Issues Market for Ordinary Shares*. Ph.D. Thesis, London Business School.

Downes, P.H. (1975). The Investment Performance of Unseasoned New Issues. Mimeo, University of California Berkeley.

Hayes, Samuel L. (1971). Investment Banking Power Structure. Harvard Business Review, March-April.

Hayes, Samuel L. (1979). *The Transformation of Investment Banking*. Harvard Business Review, January-February.

Hayes, Samuel L. et al (1983). *Competition in the Investment Banking Industry*. Harvard University Press, Cambridge, Mass.

Ibbotson, Roger G. (1975). Price Performance of Common Stock New Issues. *Journal of Financial Economics*, September.

Ibbotson, Roger G. and Jaffe, Jeffrey F. (1975). "Hot Issues" Markets. *Journal of Finance*, September.

Jacquillat, Bertrand C. and McDonnald, John G. (1978). French Auctions of Common Stock New Issues,1966-1974. *Journal of Banking and Finance*, December.

Kenny, Roy W. and Klein, Benjamin (1983). *The Economics of Blockbooking. Journal of Law and Economics*, October.

London Stock Exchange (1985). *Admission of Securities to Listing ("The Yellow book")*.

McDonnald, John G. and Fisher, A.K.(1972). *New Issue Stock Price Behavior. Journal of Finance*, March.

Medina, Harrold R. (1953). Corrected Opinion of Judge Medina. US vs Henry Morgan et al, Civil Action No. 43.757. The District Court of the US, Southern New York.

Newberger, B.M. and Hammond, C.T. (1974). A Study of Underwriters Experience with Unseasoned New Issues. *Journal of Financial and Quantitative Analysis*, March.

Reilly, F.K. (1973). Further Evidence on Short Run Results for New Issue Investors. Journal of Financial and Quantitative Analysis, March.

Reilly, F.K. (1977). New Issues Revisited. *Financial Management*, Winter.

Reilly, F.K. and Hatfield, K. (1969). Investor Experience with New Issues. *Financial Analysts Journal*.

Ritter, Jay R. (1984). The "Hot Issue" Market of 1980. *Journal of Business*, April.

Rock, Kevin (1982). *Why are New Issues Underpriced?* Ph.D Thesis, University of Chicago.

Rock, Kevin (1986). Why New Issues are Underpriced. *Journal of Financial Economics*, pp 187-212.

Securities and Exchange Commission (1963). Primary and Secondary Distributions to the Public. Report of Special Study of Securities Markets.

Securities and Exchange Commission (1973). *An Economic Analysis of the 1971 New Issues Market.* US Government Printing Office, Washington.

Singer and Friedlander Limited (various issues). *New Equity Issue Statistics.* Various issues.

Smith, Clifford W. (1976). Options Pricing: A Review. *Journal of Financial Economics*, March.

Smith, Clifford W. (1977). Alternative Methods of Raising Capital. *Journal of Financial Economics*, October.

Stewart, Percy M. (1949). Underwriting Syndicated. Investment Bankers' Association of America. *Fundamentals of Investment Banking.* New York, N.Y., Prentice Hall Inc.

Waterman, Merwin H. (1958). *Investment Banking Functions: Their Evolution and Adaption to Business Finance.* Ann Arbor. Michigan, Bureau of Business Research.

U.S. vs. Morgan et al. (1954). Civil Action No. 43.757. The District Court of the US, The South District of New York.

Index

Adverse selection bias, 23, 25
Adverse selection model, 18-41
  Allotment by lottery, 22
  Assumptions, 20
  Comparison with Rock's
    model, 41
  Empirical test, 75
  Imperfect informed demand,
  99
  Implications
    Returns for uninformed, 35
    Returns from underwriting,
    36
    Uncertainty and under
      pricing, 38
  Information structure, 18
  Introduction, 5
  Mathematics, 106-112
  Modifications to Rock's
    model, 19
  Parallel to Offer for Sale, 69
  Structure of analysis, 21
  Uninformed demand, 22

Anti-trust trial
  Medina's conclusion, 4
  Stuart's evidence, 62

Baron, 3
Barzel, 48, 49
Beatty, 4, 38, 67
Blockbooking, *see Bunching*
Briston, 77
Bunching
  Controlling adverse
    selection, 52-55
  De Beers' CSO, 48
  Empirical evidence
    New issue markets, 55
  Essential aspects, 51
  New issue markets, 51-2

Carosso, 62
Cooke, 13, 46
CSO, 48-51, 49, 50

Darby, 54, 55

Davey, 46
DeBeers, *see CSO*
Dimson, 5, 6, 77, 86, 87
Distribution, *see Investment bank*
    Empirical evidence UK, 88-89
    Empirical evidence US, 90
    Hot issue markets, 118
    Role of investment bank, 13, 47
    Role of investment bank, 14
    Test, 16, 64
    UK, *see Offer for Sale, Placement*
    US, *see IPO*

Expected revenue function, 30

Fixed commissions, 5

Hayes, 4
Herbert, 77
Hot issue markets, 116
    Natural resource effect, 118
    Risk versus return, 117

Ibbotson, 3, 7
Initial returns, *see Under pricing*
    Distribution in UK, 70
    London Stock Exchange 1960-82, 8
    SEC-Registered 1959-63, 17
    SEC-Registered 1960-82, 8
Investment bank reputation
    Monopsony power, *see Monopsony power*
    Role in distribution, 54

Investment banks
    Preferential allotments, 55, 56
    Rationing, 57
IPO
    Allotment procedure, 62
    Description, 61
    Risk-return trade-off, 90
    Syndicate arrangements, 61, 63

Jaffe, 7

Kenny, 48, 50
Klein, 48, 50

London Stock Exchange, 59, 60, 69

Marsh, 77
McDonald, 5
Medina, 4, 62
Monopsony power, 3
Morgan Grenfell, 5

New issue markets, *see Offer for Sale,Placement,IPO*

Offer for Sale
    Allotment procedure, 60
    Description, 59
    Introduction, 15
    Risk-return trade-off, 88
    Testing efficiency, 69
Optimum offer price, 29, 31

Placements
    Comparison with Offer for Sale, 61

Description, 60
Risk-return trade-off, 89
Preferential allotments, *see*
Distribution, Bunching
  Impact on adverse selection,
  58
  Modelling, 58
Purchase group, 61

Rationing, *see Preferential*
allotments
Risk
  Estimating risk-return trade-
  off, 86, 87
Risk neutrality, 19
  Implications of assumption,
  20
  Test of assumption, 73
Ritter, 4, 7, 9, 38, 67, 71, 116
Rock, 6, 19, 27, 29, 31, 66

SEC, 7
  Evidence on distribution, 55,
  56
Selling group, 61
Singer & Friedlander, 69
Stags, 104
Stewart, 46
Stuart, 13

Uncertainty, *see Risk*
Under pricing, 1
  Alternative explanations
    Adverse selection, 5
    Monopsony power, 3, 118
    Wall Street view, 1
  Competitive tenders, 5
  Empirical evidence

Distribution of initial
returns, 8
Initial returns and
uncertainty, 9
Introduction, 7
Necessary condition, 32
Uniform distribution, 27, 33
  Numerical examples, 34,
  35
Under pricing
  Distribution of initial
  returns, 8, 79, 80, 81
Underwriting
  Commissions, 77
  Estimating underwriting
  losses, 76
  Expected returns, 68
  Fee split, 46
  Zero expected returns, 77
Uninformed demand
  A necessary condition, 26
  Estimating expected returns,
  74
  Function, 27
  Rock's restriction, 29
  Test of zero expected returns,
  75
  Three solutions, 25
  Utility maximisation, 23

Waldron, *xiii*
Waterman, 13, 46